Escape Life Sucks Syndrome

Stop Life from Sucking You Dry, Stealing Your Passion and Making You Miserable

Brian Norris

53
Year

ISBN 978-0-9818612-0-3

Library of Congress Control Number: 2008906418
Library of Congress subject headings:
1. Conduct of life. 2. Self-actualization (Psychology). 3. Success–United
States–Psychological aspects

53 Year Publishing books are available for special promotions and
premiums, or for use in corporate training programs. For details
contact 53 Year Publishing by calling 414-306-0126.

For Further Help

Brian Norris is available on a limited basis for coaching,
consulting, keynotes and workshops. For further help
please see the resources listed in this book or on Brian's
website at www.BrianNorris.com.

Table of Contents

Preface

A Few Words about "Motivation"

I've been speaking to audiences on the value of living life with passion and positivity for more than a decade. I love what I do. To me, speaking and coaching absolutely suit my personality and worldview to a tee.

When I meet people for the first time they often sense that I'm not normal in regards to my enthusiasm, the ease at which I engage others, my confidence and my general outlook on life.

The question generally comes up. What do you do for a living? I usually respond "I help people to be more positive." Or I tell them I show managers how to create work environments that create more sales and better customer service."

Usually, they nod, and we go on to discuss the details of what I do and why I do it. Inevitably I get, "Oh. So, you're a motivational speaker or something? Ha! Go ahead... motivate me!"

I smile and shake my head side to side. It doesn't work like that. Although the motivational industry might want to proclaim otherwise, there are only a few proven ways to motivate anyone.

The same can be said of people who proclaim that life has no redeeming value, or that this life is "out to get them" or that life is unjust, unfair and hell bent on making them miserable. They will always get what they want from life. Their actions or inactions keep them where they are.

If you're the type of person who is absolutely convinced that life sucks, nothing I or anyone else says will change you.

So, before continuing, let's get a few things out of the way…

1. Motivation is only good for people willing or ready to change.

Nothing I say or do can motivate you or suddenly transform you or the people you care about into a successful, happy, wealthy, loving, positive, energized, focused, concerned, giving, wealthy, healthy, altruistic person.

I *can't* motivate you to stop being cynical or hateful or fat and out of shape (unless I threaten you). But I *can* inspire you to reevaluate who you are, your purpose and your passion.

2. Motivation is a warm bath.

After listening to a typical motivational speech, you might feel good. But that feeling is often temporary. When you go back to work and the euphoria wears off, you realize that nothing has changed. Worse still, you realize that you still lack the tools to do your job or to run your life more effectively.

What we need is that same dose of positive energy mixed with specific suggestions, a bucket of cold reality to wake us from our stupor and techniques to integrate the message immediately.

That's what I promise to give you in this program.

You're going to get a lot of very specific ways to keep life from sucking and to get to a place where you can see things more clearly, and perhaps differently, so that you can stop feeling like a victim.

3. Many motivational speakers, books and products are generally full of … hot air.

They say a lot of nothing, liberally borrowing stories from others and trying to pass them off as their own. Many are victims of buzzword overload, still referring to paradigm shifts, re-engineering, cheese moving, *FISH* philosophies and other concepts made popular in the 80s and 90s.

Furthermore, how many times are you going to hear the one about the ship and the lighthouse or the boy and the starfish or the room full of fertilizer before you get sick to your stomach?

Even the principle behind the book and movie *The Secret* isn't much of a secret. You attract situations, people and energy into your life every moment of every day. So it's wise to monitor your thoughts and not get bogged down in perpetual misery or low-level thinking.

4. Positive thinking alone doesn't change the world.

Change requires constant movement. Sitting on your ass all day thinking or visualizing is only going to leave your frustrated. Wishing someone would be nice to you without having a conversation with that person does nothing to change the current situation.

Praying for peace is meaningless unless you're willing to do something more than just pray for it. Behind every success story or successful person is a team of doers; people who make things happen through their actions or relationships with others.

5. Focus on the fundamental realities that can drive you to succeed more or work smarter.

Words are powerful. Words inspire. They shake us from the haze or funk we can fall into from time to time. Words remind us of our greatness and reconnect us to a world where people can succeed IF they focus on taking one step at a time and hold themselves accountable, despite their situation.

Still, reassuring words and positive intentions without works and physical actions is meaningless. I'll take a proven system and a deadline over a motivational speaker or motivational product any day.

Motivation without direction is dangerous. If I attempt to convince you that you can fly, I had better be prepared to show you where to buy an airplane or at least how to build one.

Throughout this program, keep an open mind. Challenge yourself. Go through each section. Don't just read what's being said. Think about it.

Take time to reflect on the ideas presented. Learn from the situations others are going through. And as always make an action plan for improvement.

Make a plan that's simple enough to stick to and honest enough to highlight areas where you might need additional time, resources or people to assist you.

Action Plan Template

At the end of each section you'll have an opportunity to complete the following statements and their corresponding questions. **Take the time to complete the action plan!** With each statement, pick one or two important areas that you feel will make an impact on your ability to improve your situation.

Pursuing **too many** goals at the same time is likely to lead to overload. Also, set specific deadlines for yourself and get the people and resources you need to take the next important steps. Some things will require your own will and determination, so be honest with yourself. No excuses!

1. As a result of what I've learned or read in this section one thing I'm going to STOP doing to Escape Life Sucks Syndrome is…

>When am I going to do it? (Deadlines motivate. So pick a date and stick to it!)

>What additional resources or skills do I need so that I can do it?

>Who else's support (if anyone) do I need so that I can reach this goal and stick to it?

2. As a result of what I've learned or read in this section one thing I'm going to START doing to Escape Life Sucks Syndrome is…

>When am I going to do it?

>What additional resources or skills do I need so that I can do it?

>Who else's support I need so that I can reach this goal and stick to it?

3. As a result of what I've learned or read in this section one thing I'm going to CONTINUE doing to Escape Life Sucks Syndrome is…

>When am I going to do it?

>What additional resources or skills do I need so that I can do it?

>Who else's support do I need so that I can reach this goal and stick to it?

If you have questions you can reach me by email. Send your message to info@BrianNorris.com and I'll get back to you within 48 hours.

Escape Life Sucks Syndrome Part I

What is Life Sucks Syndrome?

Life Sucks Syndrome is a reoccurring virus that threatens to destroy our business, our families and the tapestry of our soul.

As I speak and coach across the United States and Canada, I see people from all walks of life succumb to its paralyzing effects. I get emails from people of all ages, genders and nationalities asking for help.

Victims of Life Sucks Syndrome often report the feeling that life is sucking the marrow from their bones, robbing them of their joy, hope and will to live. Left untreated, "Life Sucks" Syndrome robs sufferers of their faith and passion.

In my short time on this planet, my experience and research has taught me to attempt to step back and see the bigger picture. In the big picture, this moment of fear, doubt, depression, anger, sadness or pain is a tiny dot on the timeline of my life.

I'll get through it.

Even when it seems like life is ripping the skin off of me and that I've reached the absolute bottom of human misery. I'll get through because opting out is not an option.

Asking "Why?" something happened is a recipe for frustration and anger. Good things happen to bad people. Bad things happen to good people.

Life is hardly fair or just or balanced. Victories go to the most ambitious, most creative and most thick skinned. Justice and fairness and mercy are romantic concepts but hardly applicable to the reality of life (other than your own).

Consequently, I've learned to find the takeaway (or at least the potential for growth) in almost everything. **I want you to know that life sucks only if you let it.**

Here are a few things to keep in mind every time you feel the symptoms of Life Sucks Syndrome nipping at you heels.

1. Life has more to do with how we deal with crisis than what the crisis is.

People we love will leave this existence for another. Soul mates who we trusted may turn their backs on us when we need them most.

In our journeys into the Valley of the Shadow of Debt we may get to know our creditors more than we had hoped. Sickness or disease may try to incapacitate us. Fortunes will be made and lost within a single phone call.

2. Deal with the cards handed to you or demand a new deck.

If you need to cry, then cry. If you need to scream out in rage or frustration, then scream. If you need some place to mend your wounds, then go there. But do not allow those painful experiences to strip you of your dreams and ambitions.

Ultimately, every experience prepares us for the next challenge that lies ahead. Learn to find the silver lining, the one thing, however trivial, that you can take away from what happened. Next, write down the lessons learned. Then, one step at a time, continue your journey.

3. No matter what happens to us, someone somewhere has to endure a far greater test.

Show me the person without a pair of name brand sneakers or designer shoes and I'll show you a person somewhere else with no feet.

Show me the person who hates getting up at 6 AM every morning to go to work and I'll show you another person who would give their soul if it meant being able to sit up from their bed on their own free will.

Those who lost employees, friends and loved ones on September 11th, 2001 in New York know the pain of loss.

The families and friends of the thousands of Americans and tens of thousands of innocent Iraqis who have died in the ongoing chess game of war know what it's like to hit what seems to be the bottom of a lightless pit with no way out.

How many will lose their jobs, their business, their houses, their health, their sanity this week alone?

They, like you, will also endure. Ultimately they will find the strength to overcome the emotional roller coaster that has become part of the human condition.

It can be hard to get through the tough times, but these people and countless others are proof that life only sucks if you let it. If they can get through the impossible pain, so must we.

4. Armageddon arrives for someone every second.

Even after the TV cameras go on to the next big story, the pain of rebuilding goes on.

Look at crisis in Myanmar (Burma) where 100,000 might be dead in the wake of the Cyclone Nargis which hit in May of

2008. Or the families uprooted by the June 2008 floods that breeched levees across the Midwest.

What about New Orleans? When Hurricane Katrina hit the Gulf in August 2005, millions were (and continue to be) impacted. Lives lost. Homes destroyed. A lifetime of memories destroyed in a matter of hours.

Looting. Fear. Bureaucratic bullshit. Yet, the people who remained within (or left behind) the devastated regions of Louisiana and Mississippi found the strength to go on. What other choice did they have?

Until March 2007, I lived in Broward County, Florida. In October of 2005, we tasted the "dirty side" of Hurricane Wilma. I made the mistake of leaving for a business trip, thinking that a Category One would be of little consequence.

Days later, as I drove home in a rental car from Tampa along I-5, then 75, I experienced what my family and almost a million others had already endured for two nights — total darkness. Complete silence and the uncertainty of what lay ahead.

In the first few days that followed fear engulfed us. Potentially contaminated drinking water. Gas lines that snaked for miles. Roads blocked. The search for batteries and blue tarps. Chaos as we discovered just how bad drivers in South Florida really are.

Even as I write this, hundreds of displaced families are still living in cramped 18' by 32' trailers trying to find permanent housing before the next wave of Hurricanes pummel Florida.

FEMA has no answers for them. They don't earn enough to be able to afford the $700 and up that a one-bedroom apartment costs in South Florida (and many other parts of the country).

Despite the damage, and the ongoing rebuilding, we are blessed compared to what could have been and to the ongoing losses around the world.

Across the globe, crack babies are being born. People are dying from heart disease, cancer and AIDS. The atrocities of Genocide are snuffing the lives of tens of thousands of people.

Millions more are dying a slower death with every cigarette they smoke, every fast food burger they ingest, and every excuse they make not to exercise.

5. Regardless of your status, your education, your outlook, your faith, your genetic makeup, or anything else, the physical end is inevitable.

This body will stop operating eventually. It might be the result of old age, disease, a speeding car, a slippery road, a poisoned ecosystem or an overwhelming love making session.

I don't know how it will happen. But this physical existence will end for all of us. Instead of obsessing over the *when*, obsess over the *how*. How are you living your life to the fullest while you still can?

Are you exercising your options to live fully and extremely, with passion and purpose? You control what you do and how you conduct yourself in all matters before that personal Armageddon comes to pass.

6. Someone once taught me that if you have one foot in the past and one foot in the future, you're peeing on today.

Imagine that today is all you have. Instead of assuming you have 24 hours ahead live your life as if the next 8 hours is all you have.

Will it be spent brooding over past mistakes and people who hurt your feelings? Will it be spent vegetating in front of a computer screen? Or will it be spent doing the things you've been putting on the shelf or waiting for the "right time" to follow-through on?

Obsess over this moment and how you'll live in it <u>without regret</u>. **I say suck life before life sucks you.**

7. I know that regardless of what happens to me or around me, I AM HERE TO FIND A REASON FOR BEING HERE.

We are not predestined for anything. We were born. We live. We die. What we do in between is up to us. We can sleep our lives away. Or we can change the world.

I am here to find a reason, or several reasons for being here. And so are you. In every role you perform (mother, father, lover, friend, leader, professional), you are here to find an opportunity to enrich the lives of those around you.

- To take a moment to be that shoulder to lean on.

- To give yourself permission to be an ear that hears the unspoken sadness.

- To find reasons to be the inspiration for the weary traveler to take one more step.

- To use your experiences to be a voice for those who have none.

Be bold in seeking legitimate ways to justify your time on the planet. Don't squander your chance to find meaning and influence the world. I challenge you to find the courage to live, love and lead life with passion. Even though you may not realize it, you're far too special for anything less.

Part 1 Action Planning

1. As a result of what I've learned or read in this section (at least) one thing I'm going to STOP doing to Escape Life Sucks Syndrome is…

> When am I going to do it?

> What additional resources or skills do I need so that I can do it?

> Who else's support do I need so that I can reach this goal and stick to it?

2. As a result of what I've learned or read in this section (at least) one thing I'm going to START doing to Escape Life Sucks Syndrome is…

> When am I going to do it?

> What additional resources or skills do I need so that I can do it?

> Who else's support do I need so that I can reach this goal and stick to it?

3. As a result of what I've learned or read in this section (at least) one thing I'm going to CONTINUE doing to Escape Life Sucks Syndrome is…

> When am I going to do it?

> What additional resources or skills do I need so that I can do it better and more consistently?

> Who else's support (if anyone) do I need so that I can continue this habit or action step and stick to it?

Escape Life Sucks Syndrome Part 2

The Story of the But-But Man

Over the past three decades, I've met some incredible people. People with talents (both innate AND learned) and experiences that would inspire even the most cynical soul.

Some time ago, I had the opportunity to speak with one such individual. This gentleman, new to the speaking industry, asked me for advice on how to become a successful speaker.

We spoke for about an hour and a half. During that time, as I asked him questions and gave him some suggestions, this gentleman proceeded to share his life story. It had all the makings of a best-selling book or screenplay.

It went like this:

Immigrant comes to this country with nothing but the clothes on his back. Can't speak a word of English. For a time, eats fried dough because it's all he can afford and sleeps every night on the floor because he can't afford furniture. Works two jobs. Manages to attend school to study business.

Becomes a salesman, going door to door hawking vacuum cleaners. Soon, after even more tribulations, he starts a business and makes it successful through his tenacity, sales and marketing experience and passion for success. Ultimately, he emerges victorious as he ascends the economic ladder.

I made recommendations and laid out a simple strategy for him to follow. **Suddenly, it happened, the But-But Man reared his face**.

Despite the fact that I had given him step by step techniques to enter the marketplace, the fear or psychological response that comes with virtually every uncertainty overtook this otherwise accomplished man.

- "But-but I've never spoken professionally before."
- "But-but what if people don't understand me because of my accent?"
- "But-but I'm not famous."
- "But-but what if they won't pay?"
- "But-but what should I talk about?"
- "But-but I don't have a video, a website or products..."

I looked this man straight in the eyes and told him the last thing he wanted to hear.

"You're never going to make it in this business. No matter how many seminars you attend, how many books you read, how many tapes you listen to, you'll never succeed.

"Why?" he asked

"Because it's obvious from your responses that you're not serious." I said "If you really wanted to be a speaker, you'd start giving me excuses why YOU'RE going to be a success in the industry, just as you've become a success with your business and your family."

My comments temporarily exorcised the But-But Man from the mind of my colleague. Within seconds, he unfolded his arms and shook his head up and down in quiet acknowledgment.

All of us, myself definitely included, have succumbed to the But-But Man or Woman within.

The bottom line is that you've got to start somewhere. If you wait around until the perfect moment arrives you'll die broke and alone. And if you make your decisions based solely on the feedback of others, then you should work for someone else, not for yourself.

If I had believed that there was no room or opportunity in the speaking and consulting industry for anyone under the age of 30, I'd probably still be waiting tables or working 80 hours a week as a manager of a restaurant company with no soul or passion.

The perfect opportunity is NOW. This second. Forget New Year resolutions. **What about this moment's resolutions**?

If your business is not where you'd like it to be, then eliminate the scapegoats and blame yourself. If you don't have a web site, then so what! If your marketing materials are terrible or ineffective, so what (improve them or just don't use them)!

- Can you pick up a phone and ask to speak to the person who hires speakers or trainers?

- Can you type a decent letter telling potential buyers who you are and what benefits you provide?

- Can you write a 500 word article and submit it to an editor for possible publication?

- Can you open the phone book or call directory assistance and find out the number to the local chamber and volunteer to speak for no fee in exchange for their mailing list?

- Can you write down five stories that describe your various experiences and make those experiences relevant to others (use these signature stories in your articles and presentations)?

No one expects you to be perfect. In fact, perfect people get crucified (and you're no good to anyone dead). Instead, just be your best, even if that best can't afford fancy web sites and brochures. Judge yourself according to your own abilities. No one can believe in you if you don't believe in yourself.

Build a happier, more passionate, more fulfilling New Year by taking action on your dreams and passions now. No buts. No howevers. Only, questions like "What will it take to make this happen?" and "What one step will move me to the next step (and to the next step, and then to the next)?

Finally, remember that at the heart of all good marketing or meaningful change is an idea. And behind that idea is a person with the courage to articulate that idea into something tangible. Be that person and experience a life free of but-buts.

Part 2 Action Planning

1. As a result of what I've learned or read in this section one thing I'm going to STOP doing to Escape Life Sucks Syndrome is…

> When am I going to do it?

> What additional resources or skills do I need so that I can do it?

> Who else's support do I need so that I can reach this goal and stick to it?

2. As a result of what I've learned or read in this section one thing I'm going to START doing to Escape Life Sucks Syndrome is…

> When am I going to do it?

> What additional resources or skills do I need so that I can do it?

> Who else's support do I need so that I can reach this goal and stick to it?

3. As a result of what I've learned or read in this section (at least) one thing I'm going to CONTINUE doing to Escape Life Sucks Syndrome is…

> When am I going to do it?

> What additional resources or skills do I need so that I can do it better and more consistently?

> Who else's support (if anyone) do I need so that I can continue this habit or action step and stick to it?

Escape Life Sucks Syndrome Part 3

More Tips for Getting Through Tough Times, Bad Attitudes and Rotten People

Why does it increasingly feel like life sucks more and more each day?

1. With the endless barrage of hype and quick-fix solutions that seldom work, it's understandable why we've become increasingly suspect of people, ideas and products.

2. Factor in the ongoing stream of bad news and an economy that uses fear to drive sales. Doom and gloom is good for many businesses and religious organizations. But it can kill our ability to be positive and get out of painful ruts.

3. Some blame can also be pinned on the rude, deceitful, backstabbing, spiteful, small-minded people oblivious to the damage they do to others.

Ultimately, the blame falls on you.

When skepticism and cynicism are the only tools you have to interpret or deal with what you're going though, life becomes almost impossible to navigate.

And yes, skepticism and cynicism have a purpose. A healthy dose of skepticism and measured cynicism can keep bullshit at bay, protect against charlatans and challenge the status quo.

I experience skepticism too and can empathize whenever I hear some TV or radio evangelist preying (no pun intended) on the uneducated poor, or saddened or hurting, promising them God's favor, healing and forgiveness in exchange for money.

If your life sucks don't listen to these men and women. Turn off the radio and switch off the TV. Keep your money and use it to fix your own problems (like feeding and educating yourself and your family, putting distance between you and an abusive spouse or breaking the cycle of poverty).

But eternal skepticism is not the answer. Unless you take the initiative and point the fingers of blame at yourself, you'll constantly be a prisoner to misery, bad outcomes and your life sucks disposition.

No scapegoating either. It's not your parent's fault, or your teacher's fault, or your church's fault or the media's fault or God's fault.

Take responsibility for your own condition. Consider these questions (not all of them may apply):

1. Why are you really so jaded, afraid, bitter and judgmental?

2. What's your excuse for not having additional tools beside skepticism, scapegoating and passive aggressive behavior to protect yourself and inform your world view?

3. What have you done at an emotional and mental level to heal the wounds life can inflict when it hits you full-speed?

4. At what point did you turn into the control freak, drama queen, perfectionist, abuser or consenting victim you vowed never to become?

If you're thinking, "I didn't do anything!" it's your fault too. To just stand there, or give up, or give in. To hope without taking action is a heinous approach. **Your crime is your inaction**. By "not doing anything", you've let other people or specific events take away your passion, your dreams and your feelings of self-worth.

It's your fault because you want to believe that someone else will make your situation better. FEMA won't save you. Or the government. Or the church. Or your kids, parents, friends and partners.

Even the universe insists you take the effort to improve your condition. The hardest steps are the ones you have to take when you've been beaten down.

Most of all, if you have a problem with learning from the past then it's likely your fault too.

Instead, of growing and improving your condition, you keep going back to the same patterns, same thoughts and same actions that put you into your life sucks box.

Perhaps, you keep praying that everyone around you will change. Or you expect a different result after the 15th time you went back to a bad job or unworthy partner. Those are unrealistic prayers and expectations.

Instead, you should ask for the courage to help yourself, the maturity to forgive and for the durability to survive life's land mines.

Expect Resistance

When you try to share your passion and positivity with others, or to reclaim your joy, you'll get some resistance. You'll even get people who dismiss what you have to say as "crap" or "pathetic."

Often, you'll find people who publicly pay lip service to the popular positive attitude mantras to your face, only to resort to the negative talk and actions that they are comfortable with.

Remember this. Our words, actions and beliefs are often just reflections of how we see ourselves as individuals. So when you see everyone else or everything you read as "crap" then what you're really seeing is the reality of who you currently are as individual.

Although it doesn't have to be that way, no one can change you. Nothing can help you, until you're willing to change. Until then, you'll always be imprisoned in your own private hell created by your negative attitude and belief system.

Some will even dismiss my comments as malarkey. Again, those individuals likely have self-esteem issues or a negative history that infects their world view. They either don't like themselves, or worse they don't respect themselves. They live life stuck in the proverbial mud and don't even know it.

To combat that problem, I created the **Stick in the Mud Assessment** as a way to measure how stuck a person has become. It contains 40 statements that measure many of the attitudes and belief systems we've addressed together in this program.

It goes on to help people get unstuck so that they live in the present, have better relationships at work and at home and experience peace of mind. You can learn more about this resource at **www.BrianNorris.com/stickinthemud.html**.

Ironically, the people stuck deepest in the mud are the ones with the severest cases of Life Sucks Syndrome.

For example, those who score highly (which is not a good thing) often only feel validated by insulting others or creating villains or oppressors.

Some of these people still believe the secret to happiness and joy depends on external aspects of life—other products and other people. Or that the world would be so much better "if everyone else were just like them."

Until you decide to change how you deal with circumstances in a positive way, you'll continue to remain in your life sucks prison. No one can love you or make you happy until you decide to love yourself.

One of the greatest sins is when someone insists on pulling others into their negative existence. Misery loves company. **But company loves authentic passion and positivity.**

People react out of fear, from a lack of knowledge or from a sense of entitlement. If you lash out at others who choose to be positive or others who refuse to accept your dark definition of reality, you're showcasing your weakness and smallness.

Chances are, you used Google or Yahoo or went to the Amazon website, looking for answers (or perhaps confirmation that life really does suck). If you're convinced that life sucks, part of you remains unsatisfied with the answers you've read or listened to.

What's the reason for your dissatisfaction? **The answers all require you to take personal responsibility.**

It's hardly drivel or unrealistic to expect people to be responsible to themselves rather than pointing fingers at others. Instead of being accountable, is it because you've chosen to be the victim?

If so, you insist on living a lie that says the world is against you. You want to believe that you weren't meant to experience love, joy, good health and serenity.

These are poisons of your own creation; poisons that should be flushed down a toilet instead of swallowed or given to others.

Positively Passionate or Negatively Apathetic? It's your choice. And you deserve whichever your choose.

Life is not about seeking the supernatural but rather seeing every natural moment as a miracle. It's includes realizing that the only true form of motivation is the type that comes from within.

Failing (and our ability to deal with that failure) is an important component to finding true success.

Life is whatever we see it as.

We have NO control over what happens to us. We only have control over HOW we respond to it. That truth perhaps, is the greatest miracle of all; human beings have the capacity to learn from every challenge (both positive and negative) that we experience.

My faith, attitude and perception of reality are shaped by lessons learned from my own life experiences:

- Being taunted by the other kids for being "too" tall and different
- Dad's constant discipline (physical and psychological)
- Hearing Dad say that he loved me and knowing that he actually meant it
- Undergoing 13 hours of major spine surgery at the age of 12, and being in a hospital for 32 days because of the unexpected complications
- Being healed through the power of prayer
- Learning to accept who I was and to embrace my uniqueness
- Leaving home at 18
- Connecting with the "girl next door" and ultimately sharing 15 years together

- Starting my own business

- Bankruptcy and tax audits!

- Eight years of traveling across the United States and Canada, helping other people and organizations though my one-on-one sessions, on-site workshops and public conferences

- Doing what I love 24 hours a day, 7 days a week; training, consulting, coaching and developing resources

- Learning how to keep a relationship emotionally, romantically and financially strong (despite a 15 year age difference) and seeing it continue for 15 years before we went our separate ways.

- Managing to be a provider for my family even when the clients were too few and the income was too low

- Being able to smile and stay positive knowing that every obstacle is an opportunity for growth

- Learning from Mom that even when we are in pain, that we can be a beacon of hope for those around us.

- Accomplishing and experiencing what I have while others are still trying to figure out what they want to be "when then grow up"

- Looking forward to (almost) anything that life throws in my direction.

- Discovering that no matter how weird my family seems, that we love each other and will always be there for each other no matter what

- Taking the courage to leave "the girl next door" and the life we shared after so many years (and being able to remain friends rather than living with anger or resentment towards each other)

- The lessons our breakup illuminated: 1) People change. 2) Harsh words leave scars and constant assaults only lead to emotional distance and apathy. 3) Be true to who you are – because sooner or later, a half-hearted life hurts everyone around you.

- The non judging support of my family

- The feeling of joy that being free to connect with new people and go to new places initially brings

- The realization after four months that being single and free (at least in my experience) is overrated.

- Meeting Lorraine on December 31st, 2006!

- Proposing to her three and a half weeks afterwards (she said yes!) and getting engaged

- Leaving the 180-day-a-year speaking circuit after 8 years and pursuing new dreams and occupations

- Moving to Chicago with Lorraine and getting our first studio apartment together (at just 300 square feet it was tiny but it was home)

- Coming back to Corporate America – and liking it!

- Falling more deeply in love with Lorraine each and every day and planning our future together

- The new joy and expectation of being able to connect with new people and go to new places with Lorraine at my side and being able to be authentic.

- My first Chicago winter (2008 was cold!!!!)

- My first White Christmas in Kingston Ontario (and first Boxing Day)

- Marrying Lorraine on December 31st, 2007 overlooking the beach in Fort Lauderdale, Florida

- Looking forward to spending our lives together and raising children together
- Our amazing honeymoon in Negril, Jamaica
- Moving to Milwaukee, Wisconsin (and enduring the infamously cold winters that are sure to follow!)
- The amazing kindness of Lorraine's parents

You've had moments that have made you weaker or stronger, haven't you? Ultimately, every event comes with three decision points.

1. I can decide to give up or I can decide to continue.

2. I can decide to learn from it and move on.

3. Or I can decide to permanently wedge myself stuck in the moment and stay there while life brushes past me.

In sharing some of my ups and downs and ups with you, you can see a consistent approach – hopefully an approach that you can model – to how I look at and respond to the events in my life.

Specifically I choose to celebrate the small things. I choose to reflect on what I can recover from the wreckage.

I've learned that wallowing in self misery and past failure is not sexy or conducive to sanity, loving relationships or gainful employment.

Every time you think you've hit the bottom and are tempted to start another chorus of "Poor Me! Poor Me!" Realize that your bottom is often just the tip of the iceberg for someone else.

Through the years, others in similar situations have shared their condition by email, phone and face to face conversation. Many of their stories illustrates that while each of has our share of challenges, it could always be worse.

For example, the following is an email I received from a woman inflicted with Life Sucks Syndrome:

"I got divorce papers when my dad was dying. Then dad died, lost my job. Was laid off due to budget cuts.

Am lonely. All I have is my dog. Am pretty but it just sucks being alone. Am afraid.

So you tell me what is so great about life. If you can help me then show me the light please."

Ouch. Suddenly my problems aren't so bad!

Here is my response to this particular Life Sucks email. I hope you find the suggestions helpful too:

"Dear Tina,

First, thank you for sharing. I know that you're having a hard time. If I could I'd give you a big hug and try to re assure you that things will get better and that perhaps things aren't as completely hopeless as they first appear to be.

I hope these words can provide the light you're looking for.

Because the way I see it, you've been given a lot of fresh starts.

First, you have a chance to seek out a new soul mate who fits better. What lessons have you learned from the past marriage that will make you a better wife, lover and best friend? What qualities do you now see as important for another to have before you

---

give them your heart?

Second, no one dies.

Your dad is now able to be with you wherever you go, unchained from the limitations of the human body. He loves you and will do everything he can to protect you. Be open to feeling his presence. The heart can see what the eyes can not.

Third, you may not have a job, but you do have skills. You have a chance to look for a job that pays better and that provides more personal meaning.

Have you updated your resume? Are you talking to people who can connect you to that next position? Is this a chance to update or learn a new set of skills so you can do what you've always wanted to do?

Fourth, because you have a dog, you know what it's like to be loved unconditionally and to have someone who will always listen. You deserve those things in your life from the humans you associate with as well.

Fifth, you say you have the looks. But you have to let that beauty be on the inside AND the outside. You need to let go of the fear, and love yourself even when no one else is around.

There are so many pleasures to not having to be there for someone or work according to someone else's schedule. You're not alone forever.

At the moment, you've been given a vacation, some valuable time to reconnect with your own passions and thoughts. Have you considered writing down your thoughts to express your emotions?

If you're still feeling lonely, get

dressed, put on your dancing shoes and treat yourself to a night on the town. Go to a movie. Visit the bookstore. Enjoy a coffee.

Celebrate any way that lifts your spirit (just don't do anything you'd regret doing or wouldn't do when you're sober). In your current state, turn off all the country music (or any sad songs) - they're too depressing!

Get comfortable with yourself and be open to the reality that when it's time to enter into a new relationship, the right person will appear at the right moment. Don't sweat it. And don't use your past misery to persecute whoever else wants to be with you.

But you have to look at the positive (even when it hard to see or barely there) since people avoid the negative, always gloomy or depressed person.

You have life. You can breathe. You can think for yourself. You have options. You have so many blessings that others will never be able to taste or experience.

Take care,
Brian"

As illustrated yet again by the preceding example, no one is unique or alone when it comes to sadness, loss, feeling alone, rage, or pain. It's part of being human.

Experiencing the full range of human emotions allows to us to empathize and to connect with each other.

No one is robbed of freewill either. Every action we take has at least two options:

1. One that leads to happiness, passion and positivity
2. And the other that leads to sadness, dread and negativity.

Why not choose the first option?

Consequently deny life permission to suck you dry. Look at every moment as a chance to learn, to experience something new, to be joyful and bring joy to those around you.

This perspective and attitude works for the people you care about. It will work for you too. And unlike some, you don't need someone else's permission to be happy and successful. Be happy to wake up each day able to breathe. Be happy that you can give love and be loved.

Everything else is trivial.

Part 3 Action Planning

1. As a result of what I've learned or read in this section one thing I'm going to STOP doing to Escape Life Sucks Syndrome is...

> When am I going to do it?
>
> What additional resources or skills do I need so that I can do it?
>
> Who else's support do I need so that I can reach this goal and stick to it?

2. As a result of what I've learned or read in this section one thing I'm going to START doing to Escape Life Sucks Syndrome is...

> When am I going to do it?
>
> What additional resources or skills do I need so that I can do it?
>
> Who else's support do I need so that I can reach this goal and stick to it?

3. As a result of what I've learned or read in this section (at least) one thing I'm going to CONTINUE doing to Escape Life Sucks Syndrome is...

> When am I going to do it?
>
> What additional resources or skills do I need so that I can do it better and more consistently?
>
> Who else's support do I need so that I can continue this habit or action step and stick to it?

Escape Life Sucks Syndrome Part 4

Money (or the lack of it)…

Are excuses like "lack of money" or "impossible situations" valid reasons to think life sucks?

Money, money, money. Money matters. The more money you have and the better you are at managing it, the better off you'll be. If you've been brought up to believe that money is inherently evil or that you should feel guilty about wanting to be wealthy then you are at a real disadvantage. But it's never too late to change how you feel about money.

The rich are no different than the poor in that they put their pants on one leg at a time. Instead of putting your energy into loathing people with money or bemoaning your lack of it, commit to do something about your situation now.

Here's an email I received from Jason. He wrote:

```
Dear Brian,

 "Life does not suck because "we" let it
suck for ourselves...

 it sucks because of the surroundings and
the "impossible" situations we are put
into...things beyond our control...

 it boils down to money...always has
always will...people who say "money isn't
everything"...already have enough of it."

 - JC
```

JC makes some points that at first blush makes sense. **But are they really valid?**

Is money the sole link between a fulfilling life and a miserable one?

Are we put into impossible situations or do we put ourselves in tough situations?

Is any situation truly impossible? Does calling a situation "impossible" give us permission to give up and switch into life sucks mode?

Here's my response.

```
Hey Jason,

Thanks for writing.

I certainly agree that having money helps.
Still not having money is hardly an excuse
to be miserable.

Instead, if lack of money is the reason
someone is depressed, they should see it as
an opportunity to be innovative.

For example, how many immigrants come to
this country (legally and illegally) with
little more than the shirts on their backs?

Still, years later you won't find most of
them on welfare, or hooked on drugs, or
standing on the corner with a "feed me"
sign.

Instead, many of them work and save, then
work and save some more to escape the
shackles of poverty. Many of them own
businesses, they invest in the market, and
they send their children to college.
```

Could it be that what's missing from people with "no money" is a strong work ethic or the resolve to get skills to replace ones that no longer pay the bills?

Is it possible that too many people believe that they should be spoon-fed and given success without earning it?

A popular story from the bible says that the meek will inherit the earth. **I think that a truer statement is that the ants will inherit the earth.**

Unless you poison an ant colony or kill every ant in that colony, they always work. They always rebuild. They don't sit around waiting for a break in the weather or expect another ant colony to give them a hand.

This is the same ethic we must have to be successful.

As for impossible situations, what do you mean? Many of the immigrants I mentioned above didn't even have the fortune to speak the language, but they often learned it.

How many addicts have distanced themselves from their weaknesses? How many people caught in the cross fire of the Iraq's Civil War, or the Israeli/Lebanese Conflict will find a way to resume some semblance of a normal life?

I'm not going to judge you. All situations are unique, but the question any one has to ask is, **"What will it take to lift myself from this sadness, oppression and misery?"**

If the problem is something else, then divorce yourself from the source of the things that bring you down. Break your addictions to the things that drain your income and steal your joy.

Separate from the people who want you to be miserable or want you to believe that you're trapped in your current economic or mental or spiritual crisis.

It boils down to passion, focus and perseverance. It helps to have someone or something to believe in too.

Believe in yourself - the world is an impossible place to live in for the self-proclaimed loser.

Believe in your family or group of friends who are like family.

Believe in a universe that will make it possible to reach your goals if you do your part.

I know that making money is huge. Living in most societies requires constant infusions of money to pay the bills, eat and to enjoy the physical options life presents.

The need to produce income will always be there. I've always found a way - and so can you.

Even without advanced degrees or access to a huge bank account, stand by your commitments and honor your decisions. Do what you have to do to be sure the bills are paid and that you can stay positive for the people who matter to you.

Positively,
Brian

Eight suggestions to keep money from making your life suck

1. **Do your current job to the fullest of your abilities**. In the meantime, keep your eye on the goal of getting another job or promotion that grants access to more money and more career options.

2. **Save every dime you can to pay down your debt and invest in things that make you money** (not cars, not clothes, not beer, not lottery tickets, not expensive dinners, not fancy coffee drinks).

   Seek out the expertise of qualified financial planner. The small investment they charge for the expertise might prove to be invaluable.

   If you're the do-it yourself type of person, **start reading up on the best ways to pay down your debts, earning more and investing wisely**. I'd pay for a good book that gives me skills or attend training or invest in coaching sessions that makes me better any day before wasting my money on things that suck my wallet dry.

   I strongly recommend **Money Mastery** to help you eliminate your debts and retire early. You can get it on my site (http://www.briannorris.com/money.html).

   You can also spend time at the library or even better, Barnes & Noble or Borders. Zero cost for a quality education.

3. **Also, consider a career in sales** – You'd be amazed what kind of motivation you have in a position where your income is limited only by your drive and sales ability.

   Pick a product to sell that costs lots of money. It takes as much effort selling a $100 item as it does a $100,000 item.

The upside? The commission on the $100,000 item is much higher and therefore a better use of your time.

4. Move from a service model to a product model. If you trade time for money, you face an eternity of working. If you leverage your expertise and replicate your ability to others by creating products that you can sell while you sleep, you can escape the time for money trap once and for all.

5. Don't put too much stock in physical possessions anyway. They'll rust, be stolen and let you down. Instead, invest in yourself, your family and your community.

6. Become an under consumer. Last year's model isn't bad, especially if it's been paid for. Do you really need it right now? Does it have to be new? Visit Craigslist or eBay to sell stuff you don't need and buy stuff at deep discounts.

Make a deal with friends and family to have set limits on what people spend for holidays, birthdays and other special events. It's supposed to be the thought that counts, right?

Pool common resources by sharing the costs of travel, technology and utilities. Offer to trade for services with your expertise rather than money. The worst they can say is no.

7. Go back to school to study for a career that pays well, and that you can see yourself doing for a while. Pick a career that justifies the loans you'll have to take out to pay for your education.

For example, the typical medical student will end up with up to $500,000 in student loans and various debts. This sounds like a lot until you consider that many doctors earn $250,000 to $750,000 a year after their first four years.

Consequently, they are in a better position than teachers to pay back those loans fairly quickly. Regardless of the career you choose, look at the money you invest educating yourself as a small investment that will be rewarded handsomely in the years ahead.

8. **Remember to put money aside for taxes**. Fair or not, the government gets 20 to 30 percent of what you earn. Make sure you put that much aside every time you get paid.

While most employees with a W2 take it out automatically, contractors, consultants and free agents don't often have the same arrangement. Pretend that money doesn't exist. Trust me on this. You certainly want to keep the government off you back.

Always keep in mind that "The Impossible Situation" is a dangerous myth. Few things are impossible if we dare to be innovative and follow through instead of giving up at the first setback.

You're are an amazing person and deserve to be free from a "life sucks" mentality. You are capable of so much, helping others and yourself in the process. Don't listen to anyone who tells you differently.

Part 4 Action Planning

1. As a result of what I've learned or read in this section one thing I'm going to STOP doing to Escape Life Sucks Syndrome is...

> When am I going to do it?

> What additional resources or skills do I need so that I can do it?

> Who else's support do I need so that I can reach this goal and stick to it?

2. As a result of what I've learned or read in this section one thing I'm going to START doing to Escape Life Sucks Syndrome is...

> When am I going to do it?

> What additional resources or skills do I need so that I can do it?

> Who else's support do I need so that I can reach this goal and stick to it?

3. As a result of what I've learned or read in this section one thing I'm going to CONTINUE doing to Escape Life Sucks Syndrome is...

> When am I going to do it?

> What additional resources or skills do I need so that I can do it better and more consistently?

> Who else's support do I need so that I can continue this habit or action step and stick to it?

Escape Life Sucks Syndrome Part 5

Life Suck Letters (and you thought your life was bad!)

I get emails weekly from people across the world. Here are a few more letters, and my responses. I hope you find them valuable in your own efforts to Escape Life Sucks Syndrome.

As you read these, set some positive goals for yourself and give yourself permission to move on from the sadness, anger, jealousy, regret, frustration or other emotions and thoughts you're feeling.

Replace those feelings and thoughts with optimism, idealism, and the realization that your life is supposed to be filled with happiness and fulfillment too.

The Universe gives us those things we expect most for ourselves. Expect greatness and move forward knowing that even if you get bumped, smacked down or scarred by events or people, that you are getting closer to your joy.

Life can sting us when we least expect it. Though the sting hurts, it seldom kills us. It takes work though; don't be lazy in reaching the outcomes you dream of and making the necessary changes to actualize them.

Letter #1

Natalie wrote...

"I don't know why I am writing u this but I guess I have reached my rock bottom. I been depressed for a very long time, nothing helps and I am giving up on life all together, I guess I just want to let this out on the open because no one else seems to help, listen or care.

I am not implying that u might care but thanks for reading, I hope u have helped a lot of people but perhaps I am not one of them :(

Natalie"

My response...

Natalie,

I do care.

I want you to be happy. I also want you to realize that although you may have hit rock bottom, life can be beautiful and amazing.

There's so much to be thankful for. Your education, your ability to feel, the strength you've shown so far.

I get sad and frustrated too, but refuse to stay in that space for too long. We can not afford to feel sorry for ourselves.

Part of life involves recognizing that pain, be it physical or emotional is a real part of this experience.

Pain tells us that someone is hurt or broken. Instead of numbing our pain all the time learn to diagnose what's causing it. Treat the cause.

Find someone you can trust just to talk to. In the meantime, list the little things that in the past have brought you joy.

List five goals worth fighting for.

Work on doing something every day.

Whatever pain you're feeling now is temporary compared to the life ahead.

Love yourself by working on yourself. Be as nice to the people around as possible, even if feels forced. Smile.

Find little things to make you laugh. Don't hurt yourself or anyone else around you.

Use any anger you feel to write a journal, get a job or work on some special projects.

Treat yourself to a haircut, some new clothes, and a nice meal.

Suck life before life sucks you.

Positively Passionate,
Brian

Letter #2

Alice wrote...

Dear Brian,

I am in a state of despair. I am a 21 year old woman, who feels as though anything positive has slipped through her.

I feel very depressed, alone, unsure of herself.

I do not know why I feel this way; perhaps I should see a therapist.

Words that come to mind to describe my life thus far are: unwanted (mostly by my divorced parents-and men), anxious, ugly (although many say I am not), angry (at the war and Bush), and hopeless-worst of all.

I feel as though I have no purpose, and there is no way to escape...except for my dream of beauty and riches.

I feel as though the only way for HAPPINESS is to be rich and get "fixed" w plastic surgery. Can you prescribe anything for me (drastic or not) to feel better, or best?

I exercise, eat right (most of the time), go to college.

THANK YOU,
Alice

My response...

Dear Alice,

Maybe you should see a therapist or get a coach.

The bottom line is that you have to learn to like yourself. You're with you 24/7 and that's not going to change.

If you get drunk or do drugs - you'll still be with you (and have to deal with the consequences). If you have plastic surgery - you'll still be buried underneath.

If you can't like yourself, few people will have the strength or patience to like you or put up with your sadness.

Positive, confident, self-assured people are attractive. Please don't blame your past to justify your present or future. **You have complete say in how you respond to this moment.**

Stop making excuses! About 50% of us (me included) have divorced parents. You're an adult now. Learn from them what not to do and how not to conduct a relationship.

My prescription?

A few suggestions…

First, start hanging out in places alone and get used to the joy of having the freedom to do want you want on your terms, without the approval or judgment of others.

Have coffee by yourself.

Read a book by yourself.

Go to a concert by yourself.

Go shopping by yourself.

Dance with yourself.

Sing with yourself.

Smile with yourself.

I know it's hard, but you have to accept that there are certain things you have no control over. The war is not your doing.

George W. Bush doesn't know you personally or care whether you like him or not. Get involved with a candidate who you feel has an agenda and a meaningful alternative to current policies and practices.

As far as riches are concerned, everyone has wealth at different levels. Money is not the answer - It's not the ultimate wealth. Money helps and beauty is cool, but both come and go fairly quickly.

It all comes back to how you see yourself and how you choose to treat others.

Practice smiling, saying hello and being a friend to others.

Remember that a single smile or kind word can change another person's life forever.

Find an occupation that brings you personal joy and a steady income. Love yourself unconditionally and don't let anyone or anything or any event steal your joy.

Positively Passionate,
Brian

Letter #3

Maria wrote...

Dear Brian,

I read your article on Life sucks. Things have been pretty difficult for me lately. I'm not the type of person to email anyone about my situation unless I really need some words of encouragement in this area.

I did get a bit encouraged with your aspect in life. Although, I know that life can get better. It just seems to delay.

Anyway, since I was a teenager I always enjoyed modeling, art, singing and dancing. These are the most I always wanted to do, but my Mom never allowed me to act upon the desire of my heart because of fear.

Now, I am experiencing fear of the future and what is going to happen next. I know that the confession of our mouth and our prayers will determine our future. I seem very unhappy about my life.

1. Wanting all my dreams to come true and meeting the right people to help me along the way.

2. My brothers are not supportive at all; they tend to put me down for my faith in Jesus Christ and for my beliefs.

3. I took care of my Mom for ten months before she went to be with the Lord. Three months later, I found myself moving from place to place. People are not patient enough to help you get your life back on track. Especially when you have children. Right now I'm living with my cousin in ***, expecting to find the right place to live permanently.

4. I just feel that nobody cares about me. Nobody respects my decision in what I want out of life.

5. I'm deciding to move back to F*** and see if I can start a new life there.

I need direction in life and some words of encouragement. I thank you for your words of encouragement and support.

Sincerely,
Maria

My response...

Dear Maria,

I applaud your perseverance. Use your faith to guide you in moments of uncertainty. I know it's hard, but you're going to be alone quite a bit.

You have to take it day by day, and not expect people to understand or appreciate your situation or your faith.

The only way - in my experience - to get others to see the value in your personal faith is this. Model your beliefs through your words and actions every day.

Are you a beacon of love, patience, kindness and passion?

Are you helping others without expecting them to return your favors?

Are you refraining from judging others in different lifestyles, with different beliefs and in different situations than you?

Let your fear motivate you. If you have nothing to lose then you have zero reason to fear. If you fall, get up.

At this point, NO is not an option. If you get angry or frustrated, exercise it away. Put yourself into your work. Don't take that anger out on yourself or anyone else.

Consider moving somewhere with a low cost of living too. Can you share the cost of living with a potential roommate?

What are you doing to update your skills?

Do anything (legal) that - for the moment - pays the bills.

With the experience you gained caring for your Mother, you can work as a companion for others in similar positions. Don't let pride keep you from being resourceful.

I wish you well,
Brian

Letter #4

Robert wrote...

Hi Brian,

I read your article on "Life Sucks" which I found on the Internet. You were right, I was surfing the Internet looking for a reason why my life sucks.

Let me explain. I have always been a "single" guy. Only child, only child in the neighborhood, only child in my Sunday school class etc.

By growing up alone and not having a lot of outside communication, my social skills are not the best in the world. I've always been lonely and not able to get dates.

I work hard on my appearance but I don't have a lot to work with. You know the old saying "you can't make chicken salad out of chicken sh_t"

6 years ago I started seeing a girl I had known for approx 3 years at the time (9 yrs total). She came on to me so I didn't have to make the first move and we started seeing each other. We fell in love and for the past 6 yrs have been together.

I was for the first time in my life happy. I've had dates and relationships but none of them were ever meaningful.

In Oct of 2006 she came to me and said she didn't love me anymore and good by. I have no idea why. My world came to a stop. The only woman I have ever really loved has walked out on me. Now I'm back where I was 6 yrs ago only more miserable than I was before.

Since my social skills have always sucked and I seem to have a flashing neon sign attached to my forehead which constantly flashes "RUN" to anyone I try to talk to, I have always buried myself in my work since I knew there was no hope in romance.

I have always had a full time job, and worked anywhere from 2 to 4 part time jobs daily. So for the past 30 years my days have begun at approx 6:00am and end approx midnight. I have always run away to try to forget the things I want to be able to do but cannot.

Over the years I managed to accumulate a sizable amount of money by working so much. My goal was to have 1 million in savings by the time I got 55.

When I was 46 my net worth was approx 350k and was on course for my goal. The stock market crash of 2001 took approx 250k of that. I continued to work hard and long.

My best friend and I set up a construction company He was already in the business so he and I had an agreement I would provide the money and he would provide the labor and management.

We had a couple spec houses on the market and my partner got into financial trouble from some projects he was working on by himself through his company.

Long story short, he sold and embezzled the money I had invested in our 2 spec houses. I had approx 250k invested in the houses and of that 90k was borrowed money in my name. Don't say to sue him. He doesn't have anything for me to get if I did win the case and I don't have the money to hire a lawyer.

So now my girl has left me (and found someone new), my partner has fu_ _ed me out of 250k and I'm in debt for 90k that I don't know how I'll find it. I can't continue to work the hours I have worked for the past 30 yrs as my body just will not take the stress any longer.

As far as my girlfriend, I know I'll never find anyone I can love more than I did her. So she has won life's battle. She has someone new and now she can sit and laugh that I couldn't do any better than her nor can I get anyone (she's right). She has won the life lottery and I have lost.

I know you are thinking that I would feel better if I met someone new. You are correct but so would the people in hell feel better if they could get a glass of water. Bottom line....it ain't going to happen.

Within the past 2 months I've been turned down probably 10 times when I ask girls out. (nothing new and it gets old making a fool of myself) I sit here with no ideas of how to make any additional money.

I am not real smart and have only known how to make money with my hands and not my head. Now that I am older, again, I just can't do the hours I did before.

It has come down to I have to accept the facts; I have no one to share my life with, I'll never have anyone, (I've learned how things in my life work in the past 52 years) I have no money and am in debt which I can't cover.

I look at life as being broken into 5 areas which make us look forward to another day, 1, physical, 2, mental, 3 emotional, 4 financial and 5, spiritual. 2, 3 & 4 have been stolen from me, I've given up on 5 and I wish #1 would just go away on its own and I would be free from all my problems.

Shows just how much of a loser I am that I can't even die to solve my problems. Don't tell me I still have life...that's the problem.

I probably didn't make a lot of sense but thanks for listening. Be well....

Robert

My response...

Dear Robert,

WOW! That's a heck of a story. I'm really sorry. You were smart enough to make a very complex tragedy understandable.

Have you considered things like being a Big Brother or working with the elderly? Choose something where you'll be able to divert your energies into something positive.

I know it's hard to accept, but there will be other women in your life - enjoy this period to love yourself.

When it comes to rejection, every no is one step closer to yes.

The money situation sucks too - again since early retirement probably isn't going to happen, is there at least a profession that you'd enjoy doing even into your golden years?

How are your writing skills? How about a book called "And You Think Your Life Sucks?" (just some humor to make you smile)

I know it's cliché but you still have it better than other people (intelligence, technology, experience, life, and another 50 years to become what you're supposed to be when you grow up). Thanks for writing, R.

Making small choices is often better than standing still.

I'm good at listening, so thanks for sharing.

All the Best,
Brian

Letter #5

Ted wrote...

Let me tell you some things about life sucking...

For one thing; you know NOTHING of: I was born in Kentucky in the 60's and my dad took my mom to Florida and eventually Left her ass there; with the old school rules, and I was, with my bro and sis, made ward of the STATE of Florida.

My Grandmother adopted me for awhile until the COMMONWEALTH OF KENTUCKY stepped in and then my dad took me; as convenient for him, and then the COMMONWEALTH TOOK ME again and, therefore, was institutionalized for the rest of my years until I was 18. NOW; I had to go through life being tagged as a LOSER. BEAT THAT for life SUCKING. I'll bet you can't.

My life is F*CKED at the age of 42. I could write a Biography of my life and maybe make $30.00 bucks with the people interested in some-ones ultimate downfall.

My response...

Dear Ted,

You've had some rough turns. To be part of a system for so long and to feel so powerless the whole time... I can't pretend to imagine what you've seen and what the constant loneliness has done to your spirit.

All I can recommend: Don't be a victim - at 42, you're not a child anymore. You're an

adult and you have options. If you've
decided to be a loser, then you're right.
Losers accept the negative tags others give
them. No one can convince you otherwise.

I prefer to believe that you can choose a
better role; winner, survivor; inspiration
for others; advocate for people who feel
powerless right now as they're processed in
a system that seems to reduce individual
freedoms to an aside.

If you're not going to do anything to
improve your situation, then shut your mouth
and feel sorry for yourself in silence. Stop
crying and decide to move on with your life,
one step at a time. It can only get better.

But you can't just sit there and do nothing.

Positively,
Brian

Part 5 Action Planning

1. As a result of what I've learned or read in this section (at least) one thing I'm going to STOP doing to Escape Life Sucks Syndrome is…

> When am I going to do it?

> What additional resources or skills do I need so that I can do it?

> Who else's support (if anyone) do I need so that I can reach this goal and stick to it?

2. As a result of what I've learned or read in this section (at least) one thing I'm going to START doing to Escape Life Sucks Syndrome is…

> When am I going to do it?

> What additional resources or skills do I need so that I can do it?

> Who else's support (if anyone) do I need so that I can reach this goal and stick to it?

3. As a result of what I've learned or read in this section (at least) one thing I'm going to CONTINUE doing to Escape Life Sucks Syndrome is…

> When am I going to do it?

> What additional resources or skills do I need so that I can do it better and more consistently?

> Who else's support (if anyone) do I need so that I can continue this habit or action step and stick to it?

Escape Life Sucks Syndrome Part 6

Brian and the Angry Musician

Some people like to hear that they are right, **even when they're not**. They read something that challenges their world view and the discomfort that ensues sets them off. The idea that there might be a way to leave perpetual misery behind makes them apprehensive.

The notion that we can make decisions in how we view the world, how we interact with others; how we cross the finish line flips their world upside down. How dare I suggest that life can be wonderful? Or that people deserve to be happy, wealthy, healthy and positive?

Some people desperately cling to their anger because it justifies their situation and makes their decisions, however idiotic, seem noble in retrospect.

By hiding in a sheath of anger, hatred and denial they find value in their daily existence. Their banality and insistence that life is one pile of misery is the only truth that provides the answer to the question, "What's my REASON FOR BEING HERE?"

Mark was one such person. He wrote me recently a series of emails, each insisting that life does suck and that he was right while I was wrong.

We began a series of exchanges over a few weeks. He began the conversation via email after finding my site. Here is what he wrote…

Mr. Norris,

Life DOES indeed suck. Our government is unsympathetic and counter productive to helping its citizens.

You are all alone and no one cares about anyone but themselves. Your health is forever failing; it is inevitable you will become deathly ill. We have no control over anything.

You convince people that if they just work hard and try to reach their goals with a sense of humility, it will happen, they have controlled their lives.

Do you actually think that simply "Asking the universe for what you want with a spirit of humility and expectation" will bring success/happiness?

The only thing you can rely on in life is yourself.

I am sure you would agree with this BUT you seem to think the world is a good and just place, so all you need is a positive attitude and all else will follow.

Mark

My response...

First, thanks for writing.

I agree Mark, in those absolute most essential moments, you are utterly alone.

No one can keep your family fed or protect your property or keep you from drowning but you. Not the government. Not the local sheriff's office.

It's your responsibility to do what is necessary to be prepared for the unexpected. What are you doing to improve your financial situation and to protect the people you love daily?

And yes, death is inevitable. We begin our march towards death the moment we're conceived.

Because we can't predict the day or hour of our death, we can only choose to live in the present, being fully aware and making choices that allow us to see the randomness of life as a blessing rather than a curse.

As far as control, we have little control over most of what happens to us. Life has more to do with how we deal with crisis than what the crisis is. You control your response and your perspective. Everything else is chaos. Deal with it!

What's wrong with expecting results based on specific actions?

And, no one is so invaluable that they can't be replaced. What's your point?

Do I really believe that I can get whatever I want? Yes, I do.

I always get what I really want, as long as I'm prepared to do what's necessary to have it.

And when I get too cocky or take it for granted, I risk losing it or making a mistake that proves costly.

I contend that the universe helps those who help themselves and that faith (belief) without works (getting off your butt and taking action) is meaningless.

Success takes work. The world is full of good people. They outnumber the legitimately rotten, "evil" people.

Despite the sadness and inequalities in life, each of us has the power to influence our immediate reality.

How I treat others. What I do to improve myself.

The levels at which I pour myself into loving my wife Lorraine. The effort I put into nurturing our relationship.

I create my world by accentuating the good. I can dictate this reality to an amazing degree of accuracy.

Mark, I believe in my reality. It brings me meaning and keeps me from the potential depression that dwells within many of us.

Besides, Einstein said that you can't solve problems at the same level they were created. Misery and misfortune does little to rid the world of misery and misfortune.

You're welcome to live in your world. It seems like a sad place. But hey, it's your world - and obviously it gives you a frame of reference.

Positively
Brian

Mark's Response...

I would not say my life is "sad", but it is very anger-filled. Anger is a great motivator though.

It's helped me make music and keep putting one foot in front of the other. Maybe if others were as angry as I was we could change this world and all the bad bad things in it.

Happiness seduces people to be content with abuse or mediocrity. Anger changes things.

You seem to be to be the kind of person who has the ability to help others. Why do you insist on helping people accept denial of how awful life is?

I am not saying life should hand everything to you with no hard work. But I've seen SO MANY

PEOPLE that work VERY VERY VERY hard and get nowhere.

That's the American lie... I mean "dream" - work hard, success will follow. Total BS.

My Response...

You seem to be the kind of person who has been angry for so long that you no longer see how it controls you.

I think people who channel their anger or discontent to fight injustice in the world are awesome. Anger can be A motivator, just not the ONLY motivator. Anger is far better than apathy. Dissatisfaction is a catalyst for revolution.

So use your anger to mobilize people, buck the status quo, get media coverage, blog, write music, publish books and article and petition your local politicians.

Whatever! Be angry enough to do something constructive.

But...

When anger becomes your badge of honor, the primary emotion that you use to define yourself, you become a puppet to misery.

And do you know what's sickening? People who project their internal misery onto the people, places and events around them.

Let me guess, you believe that wealthy people are evil and only poor people are virtuous? That lazy people should be handed everything?

What's wrong with telling people to be accountable and to stop expecting hand outs or hand ups?

Are you saying that people should not be expected to work?

A big part of the problem is that there will always be leeches, lazy people and poor people who are too comfortable to try anything other than succeed at a $6 an hour job.

It's also hard to feel sorry for people who complain how they have no money while smoking through a pack of $5 cigarettes or standing in the casino wasting their money on the jackpot that they have little if no chance of winning.

Even worse are people, rich and poor, who expect someone to take care of them or that welfare is their god-given right. So let's see, let's have some more babies so we can get a bigger check from the government! Genius.

By the way, how do you specifically make a living?

Positively,
Brian

Mark's Response...

What do I do for a living? I am 23 and I am a professional musician. I do charge for my "services" and I would not consider myself a "struggling" musician either.

I have toured the USA a few times and I have no other job. I'd say that's pretty far from struggling.

Best way to be happy is to move as far far far away from humanity as you can and drink yourself stupid, then blow your brains out. That is the only thing we have true control over, if we live or die. Life sucks, we have no control, and you know it.

We stand on the edge of an apocalyptic war, with a terrible economic outlook. Suffering is rampant and we can't do a damn thing about it. So don't tell me the "big picture" is worth thinking about, it's too sad. Simply taking a positive attitude will not make up for how bad reality is. Nothing can.

The 21st century is probably going to be even worse. The 21st century has been the most horrible few years I've seen (maybe news is making all more aware of how bad things are).

Obviously you've never experienced any kind of real poverty in your life. (Judging by your position).

True, people abuse welfare all the time. Lots of single mothers, the disabled and helpless elderly also use it as well. They need it badly, no matter how many people abuse the system. If you gonna have a pure capitalist society then you must have a support system.

The foundation of capitalism is taking advantage of those who can't help themselves/don't have a choice. Sure we could get rid of welfare, but the poor would probably riot and kill ALOT of rich people and gov. officials. (I can only hope)

People who point fingers are right to do so. Not all the time, but a lot of the time.

Why? Lots of people, poor, middle class, even people with seemingly big incomes have a hard time getting ahead or staying out of massive debt.

My Response...

As a professional musician do you charge for your services? Or are you able to give your expertise away without compensation?

Since you are successful, why don't you donate the money you earn to poor people? Is that a solution?

• Are you helping troubled teens learn to make a living as a musician?

• Are your lyrics designed to call attention to the injustices you write about in our conversations?

• Are you using your anger to run for office or mobilize people to vote for a cause?

• What are you doing other than pointing out the obvious problems with the world?

I agree with you. I believe we're headed for an apocalypse in the very near future - it's why I refuse to just stand there and complain.

People who complain should be prepared to at least ATTEMPT to do something about it. So, what are you doing other than crying and pouting?

Shall I cue the violins?

I bet the bartenders love you. Yeah, drinking and guns - how insightful.... Go write a country song or something.

Killing yourself is really weak and low level. Even Darwin would wince at that one. You really crack me up.

I have been poor and broke several times (so please stop assuming). But you won't hear me cry about it.

Instead of moaning and feeling sorry for myself, I try to find ways to monetize my skills. It'd be nice to speak and write for free. I'm wise enough to know that money is a necessary part of life.

Kind of like when musicians who write or sing jingles for corporate America and support capitalism.

What matters most in those moments is feeding your family and protecting them.

Speaking of capitalism, what's the alternative?

Mark's Response...

Actually bartenders don't like me, because I don't go to bars to drink (usually to play a show). I see your kinda pointing out i might be a drunk. Cute, but not true. I don't prefer the sauce. I have other drugs of choice.

The reason I included the bit about "booze and guns" was to see if I can get you to realize most people stance on life - hopelessness.

Sure, on the everyday level life is actually quite nice. But when looking at the big picture of the history of this world it's not as pretty.

As far as "poor" people not having relevant skills, this is very true. I am sure they would love to hop in their BMW and drive to their weekend classes @ Harvard but somehow I don't see that happening. PEOPLE SIMPLY CANT AFFORD IT!

Even if you get student loans you will graduate with outrageous debt. Do you seriously think that starting off your career with 40,000 in debit is a good idea? I don't.

The post-high school educational system in America is truly the biggest load of horse shit ever to be put upon the youth of this country. It is BEYOND over priced and is all pointless in the end anyway. The only thing most people learn @ college is how to do a keg stand.

Unless you're majoring in something technical like chemistry, medicine, etc...

Then it's all meaningless babble coming from professors that are living fossils BEYOND out of touch with today's job market.

Most professors today can barely check email let alone teach anything to a young person. It's a joke.

My Response...

You're right. Many professors have a hard time with meaningful answers and teaching young adults. Still, it's every student's personal responsibility to figure out how to pass the class.

Why do you ignore the fact that we control our response to the "shit" life throws at us? Maybe you need to turn off the computer and walk outside to get some fresh air.

I don't have any answers other than to focus on the relationships I have with my family and my immediate network.

And when the people around me insist on going dark, I have my personal world view, my reality, which I make real through my actions. When people inquire about how I stay positive I'm happy to share.

Since when does education require BMWs and Harvard? Are you really that naive? I went to community college. My brother got his GED (and runs a very successful business). My other brother is willing to take on $500,000 in student loans because he wants to be a doctor.

Everyone takes a different path. It doesn't take Harvard to be successful.

Education is our greatest weapon against poverty. That's why I've always advocated that local governments should underwrite the cost of sending people to technical schools, adult education courses, and online courses, whatever they can to teach skills to under-skilled people.

So someone is born with money. And that affects you how?

Mark's Response...

Other people with money DO affect me. They are the ones using us all so they stay rich. It's all about supply and demand. Markets will sell goods at the price people will pay for them.

Inevitably the rich will set prices for things, leaving the poor to try to afford it. Take a college education for instance. If the rich will pay 50,000 for it, the university will charge everyone that price - plain and simple.

All people, especially young people, are taken advantage of economically in America. This is indisputable.

My Response...

Young people have choices too. Start your own business if you can't deal with the injustices in Corporate America. Move to another country.

You know how I feel about the underbelly of marketing....

from "What is Marketing?"
www.briannorris.com/whatismarketing.html

"If you want to cause a marketing machine to implode, stop the cash flow. Get by without it. Under consume. Resist the urge to buy something else or trade-up. Return your purchase for a refund within 30 days. Find a new distributor.

Share your single purchase with thousands of other people for free so they don't have to buy it. Cut your credit cards and frequent buyer cards in half. Make your own open-source version. Create your own currency. Don't lease it. Don't rent it. Don't recommend it. Don't renew your contract or subscription. Don't contribute to the cause. Don't obey.

This kind of implosion takes the combined, sustained efforts of dozens, hundreds or perhaps thousands of like-minded people. You'll have to create your own marketing machine. Kind of ironic."

Again you're complaining but I don't see any suggestions from you on how you'd improve things if you could.

Everyone has their blessings and curses - How do you know that financial wealth solves everything? Have you ever heard of the cycle of poverty? People come into and out of money all the time.

Financial wealth solves a lot. And it puts you in a position of having REAL control over the things that matter day to day.

No money = no choices = no security = no happiness.

It's as simple as that and you can't hide from it. Of course you always need emotional wealth, no matter how much money you have.

We've already established that life is not fair or equitable or just. You're the one who keeps hoping or suggesting it should be otherwise.

Positively,
Brian

Mark's Response...

I am sure you don't care but here is my maxim(s) for life:

"Man will never be free until the last king is strangled with the entrails of the last priest."-Denis Diderot, French philosopher and author (1713-1784)

"Faith means not wanting to know what is true. There is no devil and no hell. Thy soul will be dead even sooner than thy body: fear therefore nothing any more." - Friedrich Nietzsche, German philologist and philosopher (1844-1900)

"The fact that a believer is happier than a skeptic is no more to the point than the fact that a drunken man is happier than a sober one." - George Bernard Shaw, Irish-born English playwright (1856-1950)

My Response...

I like this Diderot quote (although we don't know if he really said that) - But do you honestly believe that civilizations could continue without leaders or religion?

You and I both know that too many people like to be told what to do. And that in the absence of leadership is anarchy (as seen with Hurricane Katrina and what happened in Iraq when Hussein was removed from power). In a state of anarchy, how would you make a living?

Here are a few of my own quotes...

"Faith means being humble to accept that we don't have all the answers because we don't know all the questions. I'm willing to bet your answers will change over the next 10 years, as will mine. Your thoughts create your own Hell. That's punishment enough. Perpetual misery kills thy soul prematurely; It's why the walking dead are so common." - Brian Norris

"The fact that an angry person groans about what's wrong with the world and does nothing physical to change it makes him no better than the optimist who refuses to take off his rose-colored glasses. Both are guilty of ignorance, but the angry person is guilty of hypocrisy too." - Brian Norris (1972 - Present)

Part 6 Action Planning

1. As a result of what I've learned or read in this section (at least) one thing I'm going to STOP doing to Escape Life Sucks Syndrome is...

> When am I going to do it?

> What additional resources or skills do I need so that I can do it?

> Who else's support do I need so that I can reach this goal and stick to it?

2. As a result of what I've learned or read in this section one thing I'm going to START doing to Escape Life Sucks Syndrome is...

> When am I going to do it?

> What additional resources or skills do I need so that I can do it?

> Who else's support do I need so that I can reach this goal and stick to it?

3. As a result of what I've learned or read in this section one thing I'm going to CONTINUE doing to Escape Life Sucks Syndrome is...

> When am I going to do it?

> What additional resources or skills do I need so that I can do it better and more consistently?

> Who else's support (if anyone) do I need so that I can continue this habit or action step and stick to it?

Escape Life Sucks Syndrome Part 7

The Sky is Falling….The World is Ending…!

Since modern man appeared on the scene we've been bouncing towards the eventual extinction of our kind and perhaps the entire planet.

At this point, nothing we do or don't do can change the inevitable. The end of life on Earth as we know it is going to happen eventually. Instead of boo hooing ourselves to sleep, and living in fear we need to enjoy the time we have left.

I can tell you what will happen and why it will happen. But I can't tell you how to stop it from happening or when it will happen. It happens when it happens whether you like it or not.

All we can do in the interim is live a lifestyle that treats every moment and every person with truth, respect and the knowing it may be the only time you ever see them again..

Screw fear and apprehension!

Don't be scared or intimidated by the end; Embrace it. Because if you open your eyes, you'll realize that that end is just an illusion. It's a necessary transformation that allows us to shed our human shells and move on to the next stage of evolution.

Pick your poison.

I don't know in what order these events will happen, but they will (already are):

Nuclear and biological warfare – Every sovereign nation has a right to protect itself and to have access to the same weapons owned by their neighboring countries. This right is also the signature on the coming nuclear assault.

Who will fire first (or when) is up for debate. There are too many candidates, and too many groups who believe that the nuclear option is the ultimate strategy to demonstrate independence or to usher the return (or first appearance) of their savior, messiah or prophet.

Even Christ is believed to have said, "Perhaps men think that I am come to cast peace upon the world, and know not that I am come to cast divisions upon the earth, fire, sword, and war. For there shall be five in a house; there shall be three against two, and two against three, the father against the son and the son against the father, and they shall stand as solitaries."

More explicitly Christ predicted that just as the earth was covered in water (in Noah's time) it must also be consumed in fire. Fire (maybe a meteor, but more likely a nuclear war) will cleanse the earth and give it the fresh start for a new birth. Our 5,000 years of human dominance in the ecosystem is barely a hiccup in the big timeline of the universe.

The Zionist/Crusader/Jihadist Wars – History has shown us that extreme beliefs facilitate extreme outcomes. Those of us who believe in a God without boundaries are now in the minority. Rather than enlightened thinkers, we are surrounded by many people who believe in a God who:

- Takes sides
- Gives favor to populations that dress or pray a certain way
- Mandates specific formalized religious rituals
- And murders his own creation.

The extremists within the largest organized faiths, including the Darwinists, will attempt to kill each other and anyone who happens to be in their target's general vicinity:

- We now see many Christians expecting Christ to physically return. They are going to great lengths to force him to come back ahead of schedule.

- We see many Jews anticipating acharit hayamim. They seek a direct descendent of King David to be their Messiah. We see now an effort by coalitions of Jews and Christians to fulfill prophecy by helping all Jews to return to the Land of Israel.

- We see certain Muslims attempting to create adequate chaos to usher the reappearance of the Al Mahdi. They also believe that Esa, (Jesus) will return too, helping lay the final stones that lead to the end of the world. Jesus will kill Dajjal (the Anti-Christ) at the gate of Ludd.

- We see some Atheists or Darwinists attempting to use the legal system to advance their own agendas and religious beliefs. Many seek to erase creeds that teach morality. Many refuse to acknowledge the possibility that we contain a divine essence that Science cannot explain, patent or duplicate.

Water Wars – The lack of clean, drinkable water will wipe out millions from the planet. Many will die from lack of water. Many will die defending their scarce supplies.

Others will die from the poisoned water supply (thanks to religious extremists, companies polluting or dumping and malfunctioning or old equipment that fails to keep the toxins contained).

Bird Flu (and its descendants) – It's only a matter of time before the Bird Flu mutates so that it can be transferred human to human.

All the stockpiles of Tamiflu will be useless and the virus continues to mutate and strengthen, spawning multiple super-strains that spread globally, wiping out huge percentages of the population.

It will not discriminate by age, race or gender. One day you will cough and the next day you will simply drop dead. A lucky few will have innate genetic resistance to the virus.

Massive temperature changes and extreme weather– We already see this. While our consumption habits have accelerated the climate changes, much of the increases in severe weather stems from a bigger planetary pattern, of which the human race is but a footnote.

Many people believe that the environment will be destroyed or melt away. This is a false teaching. It is people who will melt away in the wake of the storms and nuclear winds.

While the environment adapts and reemerges from the atrocities that besiege the planet, Humans have a harder time adapting, recovering and continuing. So we're the ones in danger of extinction!

So what now? How to make the best of it...

I have thought about guidelines that every person should use to operate at the highest frequency in this life and the next. **These 18 suggestions** will help you.

Use them to guide your actions and to create a blueprint that others can model as well. They apply to every facet of your life and to every role that you assume. I believe they will help you and your community to make wise decisions and to make the most of every opportunity.

1. **Honor your commitments and stand by your decisions.**

The sense of purpose that comes with following through and honoring your promises is awesome. Commitment binds families, colleagues, friends and communities together. It demonstrates our resolve and illuminates the clarity of our soul.

2. **Respond to the opportunities you are presented with (and create on your own) to live your life to the fullest, without regret**.

3. **Love like you've never loved before**. That means loving others and yourself with passion, respect and empathy.

4. **Create clear rules for what you put into your body**. Suggestions: Eliminate white sugar, artificial sweeteners, white flour, shellfish, milk, corn syrup, and foods treated with chemicals, hormones or pesticides.

While, we don't know when the world ends, we can certainly influence the quality of our life and the functioning and appearance of our own body.

5. **Abstain from drugs or related substances.** Escapism is a lousy excuse for taking drugs. You don't need to do drugs to have a good time. Narcotics interfere with your ability to exercise free will and to think clearly.

Never ingest anything that might impair your judgment or ability to live up to your responsibilities. When emotion takes over without a chance for logic to offer a second opinion, you might make decisions that you spend your life paying for.

6. **Don't take abuse from anyone**. Love your brother and sister but defend yourself when someone tries to hurt you or put you down. In defending yourself use words that speak to their actions not their spirits.

7. Do whatever it takes to protect your family, your friends and yourself. For that reason, get a gun (and learn to use it) just in case your kind words and positive actions don't produce the desired outcome.

Have cash on hand at all times; Credit cards will have no use in the years ahead. Form a community watch group and pool resources (food, shelter, communication, non-car transportation).

8. Do everything you can to improve the conditions of the people around you, in your immediate proximity. Speak up for anyone who is put down or abused without cause. You have the power – take it.

9. Don't agree with anyone blindly. People will lie to you for personal gain. They will clothe their arguments in legalism, religious overtones, scientific justification, and ornate theatrics. What do you really think about what you read, hear and watch?

10. Don't use "God" to justify your position or cause.

11. Avoid bloodshed unless you are in clear and present danger from someone who is going to murder you.

12. Get involved politically.

Vote for and support judges and politicians who create legal systems of law that keeps these guidelines and keep the needs of their community in mind at all times.

You should run for office when no candidate exists to speak for you and your brothers and sisters.

13. **No stealing, robbery, or even borrowing** without the explicit permission of the owner, even if it is of low value or you rationalize "they won't miss it."

14. **Donate at least some of your time and/or money to worthwhile organizations that feed and train the poor**. This can be done through non-profits, directly or via faith-based organizations. I like organizations like Mercy Corps, where the no more than 5% of all contributions go to administrative costs.

15. **Fast (refrain from eating or drinking) when you feel the weight of the world is on your shoulders or your feel tempted by an addiction**. Use this time to go to a quiet, private place and chill.

16. **Remember that the fastest way to resist addiction is to remove the things that allow it to blossom**. Take yourself out of the environments or situations that make it easy to give in to those addictions.

17. **Enter into a devoted relationship with a person you love and trust deeply and find every opportunity to share your whole being with**.

When two people connect intimately and consensually it creates a conduit and provides a few powerful moments to experience bliss.

Be there for each other afterwards too. Respect and cherish one another, even when you're ticked off.

18. **Finally, remember that the end of the world arrives for someone every second**. Regardless of your status, your education, your outlook, your faith, your genetic makeup, or anything else, the physical end is inevitable.

Instead of obsessing over the when, obsess over the how. How are you living your life to the fullest while you still can? Are you exercising your options to live fully and extremely, with passion and purpose?

You control what you do and how you conduct yourself in all matters before that personal End of the World comes to pass.

Part 7 Action Planning

1. As a result of what I've learned or read in this section one thing I'm going to STOP doing to Escape Life Sucks Syndrome is…

> When am I going to do it?

> What additional resources or skills do I need so that I can do it?

> Who else's support do I need so that I can reach this goal and stick to it?

2. As a result of what I've learned or read in this section one thing I'm going to START doing to Escape Life Sucks Syndrome is…

> When am I going to do it?

> What additional resources or skills do I need so that I can do it?

> Who else's support do I need so that I can reach this goal and stick to it?

3. As a result of what I've learned or read in this section one thing I'm going to CONTINUE doing to Escape Life Sucks Syndrome is…

> When am I going to do it?

> What additional resources or skills do I need so that I can do it better and more consistently?

> Who else's support do I need so that I can continue this habit or action step and stick to it?

Escape Life Sucks Syndrome Part 8

So Your Relationship Sucks. Now What?

Make up or Breakup?

Is it time to move on or to mend what you have? Decide for yourself by answering these seven questions.

After completing this assessment you'll be able to determine whether you should make up or breakup.

	yes	no
1. Have you exhausted all of your options in reconciling your differences?	☐	☐
2. Are you communicating your desires and true feelings rather than assuming the other person in the relationship understands you?	☐	☐
3. Do you actually hate/despise this person or are you being hurt (or hurting them) physically, emotionally or mentally?	☐	☐
4. Have you considered the option that you're simply going through a low cycle that's common to all long-term relationships?	☐	☐
5. Are the two of you incompatible in four or more of the following areas?	☐	☐

a) emotionally, b) intellectually, c) financially, d) spiritually/metaphysically, e) artistically, f) patience/tolerance, g) politically, h) recreationally, and of course, i) physically		
6. Are you living up to your end of the bargain by putting in the time and effort to make the relationship work?	☐ yes	☐ no
7. Are you (and/or the person you're with) just a complete nut case with dependency issues, intimacy issues or a total inability to live in the present and to forget the past?	☐ yes	☐ no
Totals		

Now, write down the total number of yes responses & review the following questions and comments.

1. Have you exhausted all of your options in reconciling your differences?

These options include one or more of the following: counseling, talking about your differences with each other in a safe, non-hostile environment, writing down your feelings on paper, taking a hiatus from each other for a few days.

Better yet, have you made passionate love to each other until you've both passed out?

Few things create the opportunity to reconcile than two lovers lying naked next to each other after an intense session of soul to soul intimacy.

2. Are you communicating your desires and true feelings rather than assuming (ass out of you and me) the other person in the relationship understands you?

Mind readers are in the minority. And even they open their mouth and communicate what's on their mind. You have to be honest with who you are. In the safety of your partner's arms our public masks need not be worn.

It's better to risk over communicating than assuming your partner intuitively knows your thoughts and desires.

Furthermore, when it comes to relationship success, there is never a valid excuse to be anything other than who you really are.

Be dysfunctional up front to avoid confusion or mixed signals. Don't act conservative if you're a freak, and vice versa. Communicating is everyone's job, not confined to male or female stereotypes.

3. Do you actually hate/despise this person or are you being hurt (or hurting them) physically, emotionally or mentally?

Hate is not the opposite of love; apathy is. If you don't care what happens, the relationship may as well be over. But if all you feel from or towards the other person is spite, isolate the source. Work through it. Are you able to say sorry? Are you able to forgive? Are they?

Regarding the second part of the question, NEVER tolerate abuse of any type. If touch isn't openly welcomed, hands off. Respect each other's temples. Love yourself enough to walk away from people who play head games or attempt to manipulate your emotions.

If you find yourself repeatedly getting into abusive relationships seek professional help. You must respect yourself if you ever expect others to respect you. Your self esteem and self worth come from yourself. They are not derived from society's superficial definitions of status, style and attractiveness. What others people say or what possession you own should not be the anchor for your self esteem.

4. Are you simply going through a low cycle that's common to all long-term relationships?

Researchers have found that people fall in an out of love all the time. I can love you, but not be in love with you. Passion spikes up and down.

That's why we often find ourselves attracted to strangers. Love is essentially a chemical system. Typically every few years our internal chemical cycles take us through the high and low points in our feelings of love and emotional bonding.

5. Are the two of you incompatible in four or more of the following areas?

a) Emotionally

b) Intellectually

c) Financially

d) Spiritually/metaphysically

e) Artistically

f) Patience/tolerance

g) Politically

h) Recreationally

i) Physically

While opposites attract, they rarely stay together. If they do make it, it's because of a remarkable determination on the part of both people in the relationship.

Think of yourself and your partner as a puzzle with nine unique sides. To connect to another piece they are going to have to have complementary sides that connect to or help to complete you. The more connections you discover or affinities you create the better.

To assist in determining these connections, I've developed an excellent compatibility assessment. I call it the I.D.E.A. Compatibility Indicator. In it, I ask specially designed questions to measure behavior patterns, belief systems and certain universal predispositions.

When you and/or your partner are done with it, you'll know what to do to adapt to each other to make the relationship work.

If you're single, you'll know exactly what type of person you should seek out (and avoid) for a long and successful relationship. While there are no guarantees in the game of love, the I.D.E.A. Compatibility Indicator increases your odds significantly. You can get this tool at www.BrianNorris.com.

6. Are you living up to your end of the bargain by putting in the time and effort to make the relationship work?

The only relationships that happen automatically are the ones that end in breakup, heartache and regret. I spent 15 years in a relationship and often wondered why it took so much work sometimes just to keep things cool. The answer? Relating to anyone (including your self) takes work.

Unlike your iPod, you can't expect the relationship to just turn on and off with the push of a button. There will be "I-love-them-with-every-part-of-my-body-and-soul" days and there will be horrible, "why-do-I-put-myself through-this-insidious-torture" days.

If you're selfish or unrealistic don't bother with pursuing a relationship.

Additionally, are you taking care of yourself physically and intellectually? When was the last time you lifted a weight or went for a walk? Becoming overweight is usually a conscious choice. You choose not to exhibit moderation. You choose to believe that once you have kids or reach a certain age you can get fat. You choose to stop honoring your body.

Remember, your partner was first attracted to you physically and then fell in love with your insides. You owe it to each other to stay in shape and go easy on the hot dogs, beer, vending machines, doughnuts and second helpings.

People change.

You both need to keep up with culture and changing topics you can share an interest in. You can't afford to get stuck in your daily ruts.

For instance, after the great sex is finished, what do you have to talk about? Is it the same circular conversation?

Are you boring? Rocks with lips are hard to love. When was the last time you fed your mind by attending a seminar, reading a book, learning a language, or taking up a new hobby?

7. Are you (and/or the person you're with) just a complete nut case with dependency issues, intimacy issues or a total inability to live in the present and to forget the past?

Through my travels across the United States and Canada, I've met some very weird people. I've met some people who are complete basket cases, and they can't even see it. Weird isn't bad. F**ked-up is.

As noted earlier you deserve to be happy. God would never condemn you to a life of misery or guilt. Being sad or completely dysfunctional is not your fate or pre-recorded in the cosmos.

Plus, the odds are in your favor. With so many people on the planet (in your own neighborhood, city, state or country), you don't have to settle for a loser, abuser, or mental train wreck. A person who seeks happiness shouldn't have to tolerate anyone who seeks misery.

If you are the one who is the loser, abuser or train wreck, get off the dating and relationship quest and work on yourself. Find an anchor.

Re-evaluate your belief systems. Wean yourself from habits, thoughts or substance abuse you've become accustomed to.

Turn the media off and learn to feel again. Stop assuming the worst. Stop judging others or measuring people by what they do to you or for you.

So how did you do?

If you answered YES to 3 or more of these questions then you probably should breakup.

If you answered yes to less than 3 of these questions, you should salvage what you have. MAKE UP!!!

Breakup Template

Breaking up is hard to do....

After weeks, months or years of passion and intimacy even the strongest people can find ending a relationship hard to do. When emotions run high, breaking up can seem impossible.

Still, if you truly believe that the relationship is unhealthy or loveless, you must take action. Standing in place, hoping they'll be the ones to initiate the breakup is foolish.

This breakup template is the ultimate tool for people with no desire to deal with the messiness and emotionally draining task of ending relationships that should have ended long ago (or never started in the first place!).

It's also designed for people with little time or little patience for drawn out good-byes. To use it, simply go through each part (I, II, III and IV) and follow the directions.

I. If it's over, say so.

Dear _Dumpee's name____,

(Pick one or more of the following....)

   a) It's over.

   b) I don't want to see you again.

   c) Let's end this relationship now.

   d) I'm leaving you.

   e) This relationship is done.

II. Then, tell them why...

   a) You and I know from experience, that not every person we meet is going to work out.

   b) I'm just not feelin' the love anymore.

   c) You've exhausted your chances to change those bad, abusive or just plain annoying habits.

   d) Despite my subtle hints, you still seem clueless to the reality that I've wanted out for awhile now.

   e) I don't feel the spark anymore.

   f) I want to get on with your life and can't continue living a lie.

g) Things have gotten so bad. I dread having to call you every night.

h) All I want is to remove this ball and chain and move on!

i) You've become an emotional leech and I am not willing to put in that much effort at this point in my life.

j) You're so in love with some artificial ideal of what this relationship ought to be that you can't see how incompatible the two of us really are.

k) Your goals are too different from my own.

l) I find you boring. All you want to do is (explain what they tend to do)…. While I respect your right to do that, it's not what I want to do.

III. Transition Paragraph:

Let's keep the harsh words or negative battles to a minimum. I've enjoyed the journey and want to be able to look back on those memories happily. But this journey has come to an end. And because I feel this way, I'm sure you'll come to agree that you're simply "better off without me."

Choose one or more of the following…

a) I wish you success in your future.

b) I hope you can learn from this relationship. I know I have.

c) I'll be unreachable for the next few weeks, so please don't expect me to return your calls or emails or meet you for coffee or whatever. This space will give both of us the room we need to adjust, move on, and respect each other as friends.

d) I'm mailing your stuff to you (or I'll drop it off at…)

IV. Conclude

If you want to end the message formally, choose one of the following…

a) Take care,

b) Thanks for understanding,

c) Good Luck,

d) That's all I have to say

If you're delivering the breakup message in person, get up and walk away. Don't look back. If you're not breaking up in person, send the email or voice mail or answering machine message.

Then, turn your phone off. Don't respond to their emails. Don't agree to meet them somewhere "just to talk" or have a final coffee/drink/whatever together. You have to do your part to make the break up stick.

What about CHEATING?

Cheating destroys. Yet despite the obvious pain, anger and emotional turmoil that cheating brings, it happens. If it's so devastating why do people cheat in the first place?

For one, they're bored with the current relationship and torn between the certainty of what they have and the longing for new adventures. They also feel betrayed by their partner who has stopped doing the things that made them so lovable in the beginning.

Others are disillusioned by the realities of long-term relationships. The work required to keep them solid and passionate is more than they expected. Others also get angry with the spouse who gains weight or stops putting effort into how they look physically.

In the end perhaps, it goes back to people wanting what they don't have. I always contend though, that the grass is greenest wherever you water it.

Cheating First-Aid Guide

How do you rebound from the hurt that comes with cheating? What can you do to put the pieces of your relationship back together?

First, remove yourself from scenarios that might feed the urge to justify cheating.

Specifically, stop hanging out with your cheating friends. Turn off programs that seem to suggest that cheating on your partner is somehow okay or to be expected. Stay out of environments (both online and offline) that might be breeding grounds for temptation.

Second, do whatever you can to preserve the relationship; especially when you're married and have children.

Make a commitment to work through it and address the core reasons why the cheating happened to begin with.

Third, discuss what you are and aren't getting from the relationship emotionally, mentally, spiritually and sexually.

Talk about the boundaries of your relationship. Focus on discussing your sexual needs with each other.

Discuss your private fantasies with each other too. If you can both agree, have fun experimenting together. The couple that plays together stays together. But, no matter what, always play together!

Fourth, look at issues like jealousy and possessiveness.

Is there too much smothering going on? Or is there too little concern over where the other person is at certain times of the day? Is there more that the two of you can enjoy together?

If the two of you can't seem to connect without getting angry towards each other, bring in a 3rd party to counsel and referee. They should be unbiased and act as facilitator not as problem-solver.

Fifth, work on making each other happy, in and out of the bedroom. Relationships take work, and that work NEVER ends.

Sixth, forgive. I'll always forgive, because it's a universal mandate. Forgiving others for their transgressions keeps me healthy and away from the bitter pit.

And though we forgive, we don't forget. The pain never completely goes away. In time, the scars will begin healing only to open at the least expected times – it's a consequence of cheating and betrayal.

Seventh, know when to move on.

If you still can't get past the hurt, anger and sense of betrayal, it may be time to go your separate ways. Answer these questions honestly.

1. Do you honestly believe you can ever let go of the past?

2. How much time do you already spend letting this issue consume you?

3. Is your spouse so special to you that you'd be willing to work every day for the rest of your life on making this relationship succeed the second time around?

4. Are you willing to stop judging him or her? Can you? Do you want to? Or is this one way that your body and mind are trying to get you to wake up to the possibility that this relationship is permanently damaged?

5. I've said it before. The grass is greener wherever you water it. Are you willing to water it (and to deal with the occasional weeds)?

Starting over

If you're single again after a long relationship it's easy to feel out of sync. The challenge of being alone is that we can forget how to act around others or how to deal with the sense of emptiness or incompleteness that creeps into the void.

You go so long sharing your life with someone that you may have forgotten how to live independently. It feels strange. It's supposed to. That feeling will eventually turn into a feeling of rebirth, if you take the right course.

The temptation may be to find someone, anyone, just to feel whole again. Jumping into another relationship before you're ready is dangerous and unfair. So before you fall into a My Life Sucks rut again consider this.

First, before you jump off a cliff or leech on to the next person who pays attention to you because you're suddenly single, **consider the upside of being single**. What's the benefit of being single?

Single is NOT a four-letter word. The biggest benefit of the single life is that it frees you from the relationships myths such as you need someone to make you happy or complete you, that couples are somehow more normal than singles and that everyone has that one soul mate.

All of these myths get in the way of reality and affect our abilities to live an un-tethered life. More importantly being single prevents us from living passively or being content or complacent with our own development and our ability to connect to others.

A single status is as a valid as married or attached. It's your choice, and it's up to you to determine whether you have the additional skill sets necessary to make sharing your life with someone else possible.

Alone time...

How can you expect other to like you if you can't stand being alone with yourself? So before you plug yourself back into the social arena, begin your transformation by spending hours and hours going to places **alone**.

Seriously.

Start with Barnes & Noble. Then Starbucks. Then a local restaurant with a nice bar area. Then a nightclub with a dance floor on which you can dance for hours.

Only after you've learned to enjoy your own company again and just chilling out without having to talk with anyone or having to depend on someone else to give you a sense of purpose will you be ready to move one to the next phase.

This is also an excellent time for reflection. Are you where you want to be at this point in your life mentally, spiritually and physically? Are your values and thoughts helping or hindering you? How do you know?

You might consider getting my *Stick in the Mud Assessment*. It helps you to see where you are and to identify areas where you might be sinking in the mud. You can get it at **www.BrianNorris.com/stickinthemud.html**

While you are working on your insides, work on your outside too. Update your wardrobe and personal style. Be that person you always wished you could be but never could become while you were in a committed relationship.

Follow these simple guidelines to tone up and look your best.

Limit your whites! Keep foods or beverages with white sugar, white alcohols and white flour to a minimum.

Meanwhile, increase your protein intake and start a workout routine that includes cardio AND weight-bearing exercises.

Take a good multi-vitamin daily. I would also look into moisturizers that have a light bronzing component to them to give your skin a tan look. Avoid tanning booths – too much risk getting burned.

Spend some time practicing relaxing. Stress can be horrible on your skin and psyche. For my ideas on how to be beautiful, I've written an article you're welcome to read at:

http://www.BrianNorris.com/articles/yesyouare.html

Meeting People

After weeks of learning to like yourself and getting comfy with who you are, it's time to reinsert yourself. It's time to expand your circle of friends and colleagues. Now is the right time to begin meeting like minded people.

Where can you meet potential partners? If you've followed the preceding steps, you can meet new people ANYWHERE!

The only place I suggest avoiding visiting for the purpose of meeting someone to share your life with is the bar. They're a great place to "hook-up" but that gets old really quickly.

Instead, remember that professional events typically attract professional people. So, look at networking events and normal places like bookstores, supermarkets, coffee and juice bars and your local gym.

But what to do when your CONFIDENCE and self-esteem are in the toilet?

Without confidence and self esteem, life can really seem to suck. If you can't meet new people you risk being alone. I know how intimidating it can be to make the first move. But do you really want to be a hermit and shun the public?

If you find yourself going blank or stuttering when you try to talk to others here are six steps that will help you right away.

1. Get off the computer and force yourself to get out of the house.

2. Read every book you can on being assertive, communicating with confidence, and how to dress to impress.

You can also go to my main site, www.BrianNorris.com and print out some of my articles of how to have a good attitude. Once you print them out, get out of the house.

Or, take your laptop to a coffee shop with people and read the articles on-line.

3. To get over your fears I want you to start making eye contact with EVERY person you see.

Once you make eye contact, just say "hi" or "how's it going?" with a sincere smile. Practice makes perfect. After a few dozen tries you'll see how good it feels to recognize and give feedback to others.

4. Now, begin handing out sincere compliments to the people you meet. Remember, smile, stand up straight, make good eye contact and speak slowly.

5. See every person you meet as an opportunity to improve. Eventually, people will start talking to you because they'll see you're a socially confident person.

Along the way, read magazines like *People*, *Cosmo*, *GQ* and *Newsweek* (or read them online). The reason to read them is so that you're knowledgeable about popular culture and world events.

6. If someone doesn't respond favorably to you, move on. They're just one person out of billions. People can't hurt you when you put no emotional value into their words or actions. Don't let their negative attitude steal your positivity. Just keep walking and don't look back.

Part 8 Action Planning

1. As a result of what I've learned or read in this section one thing I'm going to STOP doing to Escape Life Sucks Syndrome is…

When am I going to do it?

What additional resources or skills do I need so that I can do it?

Who else's support do I need so that I can reach this goal and stick to it?

2. As a result of what I've learned or read in this section one thing I'm going to START doing to Escape Life Sucks Syndrome is…

When am I going to do it?

What additional resources or skills do I need so that I can do it?

Who else's support (if anyone) do I need so that I can reach this goal and stick to it?

3. As a result of what I've learned or read in this section one thing I'm going to CONTINUE doing to Escape Life Sucks Syndrome is…

When am I going to do it?

What additional resources or skills do I need so that I can do it better and more consistently?

Who else's support (if anyone) do I need so that I can continue this habit or action step and stick to it?

Escape Life Sucks Syndrome Part 9

How to Get What You Want

So a female friend and I are sitting out on the balcony on the 6th floor of the hotel where I'm conducting a seminar (This was before I met Lorraine!).

We're enjoying a delicious bottle of Pinot Noir. The stars are bright as we enjoy the breeze coming off the ocean. She looks at me, and I can tell she's happy to be with me.

A few moments pass and we talk about this and that. She turns now to face me, wrinkles her nose and smiles again.

"So tell me, Brian what's the secret to life? What's your secret to getting what you want in life?"

"I'm a Scorpio, we always get what we want – one way or the other." I answered with a big grin on my face

She continued by asking, "Seriously, Brian. Do you always get what you want?"

"Yes, I do," I said, I will things to happen or for people to come into my life (or leave) and inevitably, I get what I ask for."

"Really?" she said, as she raised her eyebrows. "Do tell. How on earth do you do it?"

I thought about an appropriate answer. After a minute of silence I smiled, took her by the hand, looked into her deep brown eyes and said, "Ask the universe for what you want with a spirit of humility and expectation."

That's really all there is. As I went on to clarify my response I gave her the approach I take to life, an approach that has rarely failed me.

First, whenever you ask for something you need to be ready for the positive and negative consequences that come with almost every event, especially when it involves other people.

- Are you strong enough to be happy, to be loved and to really be free?

- Do you have the fortitude to handle the responsibilities that come with personal and professional success?

- Can you deal with the temporary upheavals, tears and broken hearts that your desires and requests might cause?

- Are you prepared to live (or learn to live) in a world of uncertainty, randomness, miracles, amazing coincidences, spontaneity and perpetual ambiguity?

- Will you be able to look into the mirror daily and say to the person you see smiling back "I have no one to blame (or thank) for my current situation but me!"

These are the lifetime dues of membership. You must pay these dues daily or face going insane. Do you still want to get everything you ever wanted?

If you are willing to pay the price then you're ready to benefit from this insight (and to escape Life Sucks Syndrome forever). So, here is the secret again...

Ask the universe for what you want with a spirit of humility and expectation.

Don't get cocky with the universe. Humility demands that you manage or altogether eliminate your ego.

Humility demands that you learn something new from every person you meet and every event you experience.

Humility requires that you actively improve your mind daily (reading, watching or listening, classes, internships, workshops, volunteering to take on new projects outside your written job description, job shadowing) and that you apply your newly acquired knowledge whenever possible.

With this spirit of humility specify what you want to happen. I usually close my eyes and speak my expectation as if I'm talking to a friend. You can also write down your expectation. Read what you've written out loud.

Be descriptive when you tell the universe what you want. Share details of the events you want to happen or the people you want to meet. See the colors. Smell the aromas and distinct fragrances that you will encounter when your expectation comes to pass. Experience the emotions. Note the time of day you want this to happen and all the miniscule details.

Do all of this with the foundational understanding that while you'll get what you asked for (often within hours or days), it won't be in the linear order or specific process or exact package that you imagined.

Thank the universe for hearing, processing and responding to your request. Now, keep your eyes, heart, mind and options open.

Remember how I wrote about being prepared to live (or learn to live) in a world of uncertainty, randomness, miracles, amazing coincidences, spontaneity and perpetual ambiguity? Well, this is the world you're in now.

Don't write anything or anyone off as insignificant. Almost everything that happens to you (and the people you meet) after you've made your request is somehow a manifestation of events set into motion by your expectation.

Don't overanalyze; just go with it. The fragments don't always make intrinsic sense by themselves. Hindsight is the filter through which the pieces will finally make sense, so exercise good judgment and then enjoy the moment.

Equally important, plan actions that will create an environment where the universe can assist you.

For example, don't just sit in your home or office waiting for the phone to ring. Make some phone calls. Send out some emails or text messages. Go to places that you truly believe will put you in touch with people that can assist you (and where you can assist them) in reaching your goals.

When you go somewhere, initiate conversations rather than waiting for someone to approach you. It doesn't matter what your gender, age or status is. You have to take initiative.

Be clear and specific about what you'd like to happen or do. Listen to what is being said. Pay attention to the non-verbal cues you get from others too. The key is to expect the best of every opportunity without being overly pushy or needy. **There's a thick line between freak and friendly!**

Ask how you can be of service to others too (it is part of being humble). Reciprocity, when it comes from a place of kindness or positivity is an amazing dynamic. Give freely. Receive freely.

Ask for the job, the meeting, the phone number, the kiss, the date, whatever. The worst that can happen in any situation is to be met with a "No" or "Not right now."

But if you don't ask or do nothing to capitalize on your circumstances you don't get. I expect a yes, and if I've learned as much as I can and taken actions to create the ideal conditions, I generally get the yes (and much more).

The fine print here is that we get what we focus on as long as we:

1. trust the universe to deliver

2. can relinquish our need to **control** the process

3. inwardly smile and remain positively passionate in knowing the outcome will be what we needed

Are you ready? You deserve everything you get, everything you want, and everything you need. Just ask for it, and do what you need to do to make your desires and dreams a reality.

Part 9 Action Planning

1. As a result of what I've learned or read in this section one thing I'm going to STOP doing to Escape Life Sucks Syndrome is...

> When am I going to do it?

> What additional resources or skills do I need so that I can do it?

> Who else's support do I need so that I can reach this goal and stick to it?

2. As a result of what I've learned or read in this section one thing I'm going to START doing to Escape Life Sucks Syndrome is...

> When am I going to do it?

> What additional resources or skills do I need so that I can do it?

> Who else's support do I need so that I can reach this goal and stick to it?

3. As a result of what I've learned or read in this section one thing I'm going to CONTINUE doing to Escape Life Sucks Syndrome is...

> When am I going to do it?

> What additional resources or skills do I need so that I can do it better and more consistently?

> Who else's support do I need so that I can continue this habit or action step and stick to it?

Parting Words...

First, congratulations. You now have the tools you need to escape Life Sucks Syndrome for good. Life rocks; if you know how to deal with stuff it throws at you.

Review each section again. This time, stop along the way to answer the questions that deal with the issues you're facing. Decide to rise above the anger, the depression, the sadness, or the apathy you might be feeling. Succeed in spite of the inequalities of the system.

Protect yourself from people who try to steal your joy. Stop complaining. Instead, start doing something meaningful about the things that irk you. Make up your own rules. Escape your captivity. You can do it.

If after considering all you've read you still choose to believe that life sucks, then at least you took a stand on something. That, in a warped way, is progress. Perhaps misery suits you.

In choosing to wallow in your own misery, you're just responding like many people who remain plugged into the constant flow of negative news and violent images.

Many people are addicted to misery, anxiety, fear (blame it on your Amygdala). Perhaps, you too are addicted to the stability that misery and pessimism brings you. Perhaps you love the rationalizations you can make thanks to your perpetual misery. Your violin is set to auto play.

If you choose to believe that this misery and depression is all there is to life, you're standing in a long line of mediocrity.

You've justified your perspective and bought into society's idea of how you ought to live or feel. You've written your game plan and in the process, extinguished the flames of possibility.

Miserable people, events, music, and circumstances got to you, and now you're just like them. You've rejected your highest potential and chosen to be a bottom feeder.

Remember what we said earlier, misery loves company.

Try this. Spend **one day** pretending to be happy and passionate. Observe how fast the miserable people in your life try to strip you of the joy you seem to have with their word and actions!

They want you to be miserable like them all the time. They need affirmation that it's everyone else's fault and that they are being unfairly persecuted because they're different. Anything else challenges the reality they've created for themselves!

Ultimately, maybe we're just operating from different playbooks.

If you **want** life to stop sucking, you have to choose something outside of the pre-fabricated templates you've accepted as doctrine for so long.

Don't be afraid of standing out or demonstrating what a life free from Life Suck Syndrome looks and feels like.

Embrace the possibilities that come with a life without limits. Connect with every person you meet by modeling passion and positivity. Thrive on passion and on your right to choose joy.

About the Author

A bestselling author and professional speaker, Brian Norris is a leading expert on living with passion and positivity.

Brian helps individuals and organizations to leverage the awesome power of passion and positivity to solve problems creatively and build great relationships.

In addition to *Escape Life Sucks Syndrome*, Brian authored The *Stick in the Mud Assessment*, a quick and to the point personal assessment that shows people how to be happier, healthier and more positive.

Brian is also the creator of the *Positively Passionate Creed*, the basis of a complete coaching programs used by thousands to guide them through life.

Since 1995 Brian Norris has traveled to all 50 US states at least five times speaking, coaching and consulting. He has presented over 10,000 hours of training and hundreds of keynotes to 50,000+ people representing thousands of organizations.

You can reach Brian Norris by emailing info@BrianNorris.com. Or visit BrianNorris.com for articles and additional resources.

The Positively Passionate Creed

By Brian Norris

While I honor my commitments and stand by my decisions, I will not forfeit my right to experience life's random possibilities.

I savor each moment completely and to its highest potential. **That's why I live in the present** – I know that this event, this opportunity, this chance to connect soul-to-soul may not happen again.

I own my choices and refuse to blame others for my economics, my mindset, my health or my self-worth. Instead, **I hold myself accountable**. I use lessons learned to make smarter choices. I create options where none seem to exist.

I will not surrender to mediocrity. I question the status quo. **I embrace my power to change my world for the better** one conversation, one idea, one decision and one moment of unsolicited positivity at a time.

I give myself permission to live beyond my stereotype and programming, without regret. I give to, and take from the positive energy and endless miracles that surround me.

For these reasons, I am positively passionate... all the time.

Notes